14 Feb 2023

MW01062417

The
Doctrine
of
CHRIST

Guide to
Bible Doctrine

The
Doctrine
of
CHRIST

Norman L. Geisler
Douglas E. Potter

Indian Trail, North Carolina

The Doctrine of Christ
NGIM Guide to Bible Doctrine, Volume 3
Norman L. Geisler and Douglas E. Potter

Copyright © 2016 Norman L. Geisler

Published by Norm Geisler International Ministries | P.O. Box 2638 | Indian Trail,
NC 28079 | USA
www.ngim.org

Printed in the United States of America

ISBN–13: 978–1539375548
ISBN–10: 1539375544

Contents

Introduction

The apostle Paul clearly showed the deep practical theological importance of knowing and studying Jesus Christ when he wrote,

> Have this attitude in yourselves which was also in Christ Jesus, who, although He existed in the form of God, did not regard equality with God a thing to be grasped, but emptied Himself, taking the form of a bond–servant, and being made in the likeness of men. (Phil. 2:5–7)

The study of the doctrine of Christ is central to the Christian faith. Long technical treaties on this doctrine while important, can be intimidating to the Christian that wants to dig into the study for the first time. Even some less technical approaches might not state the doctrine in as systematic or comprehensive manner as it should. As a result those new to the study of this doctrine may never be exposed to important concepts and issues.

Christians, more than ever, need a study of Jesus Christ that is true and systematic. Many in and outside the church do not understand how this doctrine is formulated, how it intersects and informs many areas of Christian thought and life which serves as a foundation to a Christian worldview.

This book is a popular introduction to the study of Christ firmly rooted in the evangelical tradition. Each chapter covers an area of the doctrine of Christ, stresses its basis, doctrinal importance and interconnectedness to formulating a Christian view of Jesus Christ and other doctrines. The study questions provided help reinforce the material and make it usable even for a formal study of Christ. It is ideal for personal study or in groups for the home, church, school or ministry environment.

The approach is faithful to the historical evangelical position that integrates all truth as God's truth and upholds the classical view of the full inspiration and inerrancy of the Bible.

Dr. Norman L. Geisler has taught theology and Bible doctrine in churches, colleges, and seminaries for over 60 years. Having authored many works in Christian apologetics and theology (*Systematic Theology In One Volume*), this work, while maintaining the precision and comprehensiveness the study needs, uniquely makes it accessible to everyone.

Dr. Douglas E. Potter is an assistant professor and Director of the Doctor of Ministry program at Southern Evangelical Seminary. He has been teaching Christian theology and apologetics for over a decade and is an author or co–author for several books.

1

The Preincarnate Christ

In the beginning was the Word, and the Word was with
God, and the Word was God. He was in the beginning
with God. All things came into being through Him, and
apart from Him nothing came into being that has come
into being.
John 1:1–3

Our study of the Doctrine of Christ, also known as Christology, begins with Jesus' Preincarnate state. This is established by examining the eternal sonship of Jesus Christ as expressed in the Old and New Testament. This is followed by His Preincarnate appearances as the Messenger of Yahweh in the Old Testament prior to His permanent incarnation and virgin birth (Chapter 2).

CHRIST'S ETERNAL SONSHIP

The title "Son of God" entails that Jesus Christ is of the order of God (John 3:16–17). Hence Christ is the eternal Son of God which is clear from both the Old and New Testaments. As Son, He is eternally submissive to the will of the Father to be the redeemer of humankind (Heb. 10:7–10) while on earth (John 15:10) and in eternity to come (1 Cor. 15:24–28). Both the Old (Ps. 2:6–8, 12) and New (John 1:1, 17:5; Col. 1:16–17) Testaments affirm Christ's Eternal Sonship.

Christ's Eternal Sonship in the Old Testament

The Old Testament speaks of the eternal Son. Psalm 2:6–8, 12 (cf. Prov. 30:4) says,

> I have installed My King Upon Zion, My holy mountain. I will surely tell of the decree of the Lord: He said to Me, 'You are My Son, Today I have begotten You. Ask of Me, and I will surely give the nations as Your inheritance, And the very ends of the earth as Your possession. . . . Do homage to the Son, that He not become angry, and you perish in the way, For His wrath may soon be kindled. How blessed are all who take refuge in Him!

Isaiah wrote, "Therefore the Lord Himself will give you a sign: Behold, a virgin will be with child and bear a son, and she will call His name Immanuel [i.e., "God with us"] (Isa. 7:14). Isaiah also wrote "For a child will be born to us, a son will be given to us; And the government will rest on His shoulders; And His name will be called Wonderful Counselor, Mighty God, Eternal Father, Prince of Peace" (Isa. 9:6).

Christ's Eternal Sonship in the New Testament

The New Testament makes it clear that the second person of the Trinity, Christ the Son of God, had no beginning. John says, "In the beginning was the Word, and the Word was with God, and the Word was God" (John 1:1). He is before creation since "All things came into being through Him, and apart from Him nothing came into being that has come into being" (John 1:3).

The Apostle Paul said, "For by Him all things were created, both in the heavens and on earth, visible and invisible, whether thrones or dominions or rulers or authorities—all things have been created through Him and for Him. He is before all things, and in Him all things hold together" (Col. 1:16–17).

Jesus prayed, "Now, Father, glorify Me together with Yourself, with the glory which I had with You before the world was" (John 17:5). He even claimed, "Jesus said to them, "Truly, truly, I say to you, before Abraham was born, I am" (John 8:58). That Christ claimed to be the eternal Son of the eternal Father, is clear when He said,

> "I and the Father are one." . . . The Jews picked up stones again to stone Him. Jesus answered them, "I showed you many good works from the Father; for which of them are you stoning Me?" The Jews answered Him, "For a good work we do not stone You, but for blasphemy; and because You, being a man, make Yourself out to be God." (John 10:30, 33)

As Son, He is eternally submissive to the Father. From eternity past, the Son of God is willing to submit to the will of the Father to be the Redeemer of humankind. The author of Hebrews records Jesus proclamation:

> "Then I said, 'Behold, I have come (In the scroll of the book it is written of Me) To do Your will, O God.'" After saying above, "Sacrifices and offerings and whole burnt offerings and sacrifices for sin You have not desired, nor have You taken pleasure in them" . . . then He said, "Behold, I have come to do Your will." He takes away the first in order to establish the second. By this will we have been sanctified through the offering of the body of Jesus Christ once for all. (Heb. 10:7–10)

On earth, Christ always obeyed the will of the Father, He said, "I have kept My Father's commandments and abide in His love. (John 15:10). Paul said of Christ,

> Have this attitude in yourselves which was also in Christ Jesus, who, although He existed in the form of God, did not regard equality with God a thing to be grasped but emptied Himself, taking the form of a bond–servant, and being made in the likeness of men. Being found in appearance as a man, He humbled Himself by becoming obedient to the point of death, even death on a cross. (Phil. 2:5–8)

Paul also records that in eternity to come, Christ will still submit to the Father,

> Then comes the end, when He hands over the kingdom to the God and Father, when He has abolished all rule and all authority and power. For He must reign until He has put all His enemies under His feet. The last enemy that will be abolished is death. For He has put all things in subjection under His feet. But when He says, "All things are put in subjection," it is evident that He is excepted who put all things in subjection to Him. When all things are subjected to Him, then the Son Himself also will be subjected to the One who subjected all things to Him, so that God may be all in all. (1 Cor. 15:24–28)

Hence, it is clear that Christ is the *eternal* Son of God from both the Old and New Testament. As such He is always submissive to the Father in eternity as well as on earth.

CHRIST AS THE MESSENGER OF YAHWEH IN THE OLD TESTAMENT

One of the strongest indicators of Christ's preincarnate sonship and deity in the Old Testament is His appearance as "the Angel [Messenger] of the Lord." The term

"Yahweh" (Lord) is used exclusively of God in the Old Testament. Isaiah 45:18 says,

> For thus says the Lord, who created the heavens (He is the God who formed the earth and made it, He established it and did not create it a waste place, but formed it to be inhabited), "I am the Lord [Yahweh], and there is none else.

Yahweh even appeared to the patriarchs. Exodus 6:2–3 says, "I am the Lord [Yahweh], and I appeared to Abraham, Isaac, and Jacob, as God Almighty, but by My name, Lord, I did not make Myself known to them."

That Jesus Christ is the Messenger of Yahweh in the Old Testament is supported by the following.

The Messenger of the Lord is Yahweh

One of the messengers (angels) who appeared to Abraham was called "the Lord" [Yahweh] in Genesis 18:1. In Genesis 18:22 it says "Then the men turned away from there and went toward Sodom, while Abraham was still standing before the Lord [Yahweh]."

He also appeared to Moses. Exodus 3:2 says, "The angel of the Lord [Yahweh] appeared to him in a blazing fire from the midst of a bush; and he looked, and behold, the bush was burning with fire, yet the bush was not consumed." He is called "the Lord" [Yahweh] (cf. v. 8) who gives His name as "I AM WHO I AM" (v. 14).

The angel of the Lord appeared to Manoah's wife in Judges 13:3: "Then the angel of the Lord appeared to the woman and said to her, 'Behold now, you are barren and have borne no children, but you shall conceive and give birth to a son.' " Manoah prayed to the Lord [Yahweh] in Judges 13:8: "Then Manoah entreated the Lord and said, 'O Lord [Yahweh], please let the man of God whom You have sent come to us again that he may teach us what to do for the boy who is to be born." When asked His name, he replied "Wonderful" (Judges 13:18; cf. Isa. 9:6).

It is also clear that the Angel of the Lord is a different Person than the Lord. Zechariah 1:12–13 says, "Then the angel of the Lord said, 'O Lord of hosts, how long will You have no compassion for Jerusalem and the cities of Judah, with which You have been indignant these seventy years?' The Lord answered the angel who was speaking . . ."

This same kind of conversation takes place in Psalm 110:1: "The Lord [Yahweh] says to my Lord [Adonai]: "Sit at My right hand Until I make Your enemies a footstool for Your feet" (cf. Ps. 45). Jesus used this as an argument for His Messiahship against the Pharisees (Matt. 22:42–45; Heb. 1:8).

The Angel of the Lord is Christ

That the Angel of the Lord, described in the Old Testament, is Christ, the second person of the Trinity is based on two lines of evidence. First, The Angel of the Lord in the Old Testament serves the same role as does Christ in the New Testament (Isa. 63:7–10). The Father plans and sends the Son who is the Redeemer, and the Holy Spirit is the one who convicts and applies redemption to the redeemed. Isaiah even provides a description, of all three members of the Godhead:

> I will tell of the kindnesses of the LORD, the deeds for which he is to be praised, according to all the LORD [Father] has done for us . . . and so he became their Savior [Son]. In all their distress he too was distressed, and the angel of his presence saved them. In his love and mercy he redeemed them; . . . Yet they rebelled and grieved his Holy Spirit [the Spirit]." (Isa. 63:7–10)

Second, once the Son (Christ) came in permanent incarnate form (John 1:1, 14), never again does *the* Angel of the Lord appear. Angels appear (cf. Acts 12:7f.). But no angel appears that commands or accepts worship. No angel that claims to be God appears ever again. Other appearances of the Preincarnate Christ that do not use the description the Angel of the Lord, also gives evidence to this line of reasoning (Josh. 5:13–14).

The Father and Holy Spirit never appear as a human in Scripture. Hence, we can state that Jesus Christ, as a person, eternally existed and appeared as a man before His vaginal conception on earth.

SUMMARY

Both the Old and New Testament give witness to the fact that Jesus Christ is the eternal Son of God. As such, Jesus Christ appeared as a man before His incarnation (Preincarnate) as the Angel or Messenger of the Lord in the Old Testament. The Angel of the Lord is recognized as Yahweh [God] and serves the role as Christ in the Old Testament. Furthermore, all appearances of *the* Angel of the Lord cease after the Son of God permanently became incarnate and was born of the virgin Mary (John. 1:1; 14).

Questions to Answer

1. Why is it important to demonstrate that Jesus is the enteral Son of God?
2. What biblical versus, from the Old and New Testaments, support the eternal Sonship of Jesus Christ?
3. How do we know that the Angel of the Lord is Yahweh?
4. What biblical verses support the Preincarnate Christ?
5. What is the significance of the Preincarnate Christ being designated The Angel of the Lord?

2

The Virgin Birth of Christ

Mary said to the angel, "How can this be, since I am a virgin?" The angel answered and said to her, "The Holy Spirit will come upon you, and the power of the Most High will overshadow you; and for that reason the holy Child shall be called the Son of God.
Luke 1:34–35

The Virgin Birth is the miraculous conception of Christ in the virgin's womb. Our study covers its anticipation in the Old Testament and its explicit basis in the New Testament. Its truth is foundational to the study of Jesus Christ. If Jesus was not virgin born then he would be a sinner like everyone else. His virgin conception ensured He would not inherit a sin nature and is therefore essential to His sinlessness.

Christ's Virgin Birth

Old Testament Anticipation of the Virgin Birth

The Old Testament contains Messianic prophecies that implicitly and explicitly anticipate the virgin birth.

Genesis 3:15 says, "And I will put enmity between you and the woman, and between your seed and her seed; He shall bruise you on the head, And you shall bruise him on the heel." The Redeemer coming from the "offspring" or "seed" of the women is important. Descendants are normally traced through their father (Gen. 5) and this is even done for the Messiah (Matt. 1). Hence, by "seed of the women" it is implicit that the Messiah would not have a natural father, and thus be virgin–born.

The virgin birth is also implied in the curse, that no offspring of Jeconiah will sit on the throne of David or rule Judah (Jer. 22:30). Jeconiah is in the fatherly line of Jesus (Matt. 1:12). But since Joseph was only Jesus' legal father (by virtue of being engaged to Mary when she became pregnant) and Jesus was the actual son of David through Mary (Luke 3), Jesus did not inherit this curse by virtue of His virgin birth.

The virgin birth is explicitly predicted in Isaiah 7:14: "Therefore the Lord Himself will give you a sign: Behold, a virgin will be with child and bear a son, and she will call His name Immanuel." The whole context of Isaiah 7–11 forms an unbreakable chain of messianic prophecy (cf. Isa. 7:14; 8:8; 9:6; 11:1–5). The New Testament interprets Isaiah 7:14 as prophetic to indicate that it might be fulfilled (Matt. 1:22) and to show the supernaturalness of the birth and deity of Christ (Matt. 1:23). Some have argued that the Hebrew word (*almah*) translated "virgin" in this passage should be translated "young woman." However, there are several reasons against this. First, there are no examples in the Old Testament where the Hebrew word (*almah*) means anything but a young unmarried girl. Since, she was to conceive and bare the child as a virgin, it cannot refer to a natural conception. Second, the Hebrew term for a young unmarried girl (*bethulah*) was not used here because it is used of a married person (Joel 1:8). Third, the Greek Old Testament (LXX) as well as the New Testament when citing Isaiah 7:14 translate *almah* as "virgin." Finally, the text clearly says that both the conception and birth were by a virgin, which would not be true if it was a natural birth. To translate it any other way, such as a young married women who conceives, is to deny that it refers to a virgin which is contrary to Isaiah 7:14.

Others object saying that the prophecy of this passage is fulfilled in the natural birth of Maher–Shalal–Hash–Baz of Isaiah 8:3. However, there are dimensions of this prophecy that could only apply to Christ. First, the one born of a virgin is called "Immanuel" (God with us). As quoted in the New Testament (Matt. 1:23) this is a reference to the deity of Christ. Second, the prediction is to the whole "house of David" (Isa. 7:13). Therefore, it cannot be limited to any natural birth in Isaiah's day. Third, there is an emphasis on this being a wonderful unheard–of "sign" (Isa. 7:11–14). As such, it is best used to explain the supernatural birth of Christ, not just to the natural birth of Maher–Shalal–Hash–Baz. Otherwise, we are left with the impossible task of answering why an ordinary birth should be understood as an extraordinary sign. Finally, one and the same verse cannot refer to the birth of Maher–Shalal–Hash–Baz in Isaiah's day and Jesus Christ. Otherwise, Maher–Shalal–Hash–Baz was virgin born and Christ was not—the same verse cannot mean two different (opposing) things. Given that the inspired New Testament applies this verse to the virgin birth of Christ, we must take it as referring to Jesus Christ.

New Testament Basis for the Virgin Birth

While some of the Old Testament is implicit, the New Testament clearly affirms that Chrsit was born of a virgin Matthew 1:18–23 says,

> Now the birth of Jesus Christ was as follows: when His mother Mary had been betrothed to Joseph, before they came together she was found to be with child by the Holy Spirit. And Joseph her husband, being a righteous man and not wanting to disgrace her, planned to send her away secretly. But when he had considered this, behold, an angel of the Lord appeared to him in a dream, saying, "Joseph, son of David, do not be afraid to take Mary as your wife; for the Child who has been conceived in her is of the Holy Spirit. She will bear a Son; and you shall call His name Jesus, for He will save His people from their sins." *Now all this took place to fulfill what was spoken by the Lord through the prophet: "Behold, the virgin shall be with child and shall bear a Son, and they shall call His name Immanuel,"* which translated means, "God with us." (Emphasis added)

Matthew 1:18–23 (cf. Luke 1:26–35) contains four factors demonstrating Christ's Virgin Birth: 1) Mary conceived "before they came together" so it was not a natural conception. 2) Joseph's reaction "he had in mind to divorce her" reveals he had no sexual relations with Mary. 3) The event was supernatural "what is conceived in her is of the Holy Spirit." 4) the sections from the prophet cited about a "virgin" giving "birth" to a child indicates that she had no sexual relations with anyone before, during, and after He was conceived–even when He was born.

Luke (1:26–35), likewise, gives detailed attention to these areas in the announcement of Christ's virgin birth.

> Now in the sixth month the angel Gabriel was sent from God to a city in Galilee called Nazareth, to a

virgin engaged to a man whose name was Joseph, of the descendants of David; and the virgin's name was Mary. And coming in, he said to her, "Greetings, favored one! The Lord is with you." But she was *very perplexed* at this statement, and kept pondering what kind of salutation this was. The angel said to her, "Do not be afraid, Mary; for you have found favor with God. And behold, you will conceive in your womb and bear a son, and you shall name Him Jesus. He will be great and will be called the Son of the Most High; and the Lord God will give Him the throne of His father David; and He will reign over the house of Jacob forever, and His kingdom will have no end." Mary said to the angel, "How can this be, since I am a virgin?" The angel answered and said to her, "*The Holy Spirit will come upon you, and the power of the Most High will overshadow you*; and for that reason the holy Child shall be called the Son of God. (Emphasis added)

Luke also demonstrates the supernatural conception of Christ. Mary's reaction of being perplexed and afraid shows she knew she was a virgin. Conception is from "the Power of the Most High." Mary's song/meditation on the event shows she knew it was supernatural.

Luke's record (2:4–19) of the actual birth of Christ gives further indication that it was a virgin birth.

Joseph also went up from Galilee, from the city of Nazareth, to Judea, to the city of David which is called Bethlehem, because he was of the house and family of David, in order to register *along with Mary, who was engaged to him, and was with child*. . . . In the same region there were some shepherds staying out in the fields and keeping watch over their flock by night. And *an angel of the Lord suddenly stood before them*, and the glory of the Lord shone around them; and they were terribly frightened. But the angel said to them, "Do not be afraid; for behold, I bring you good news of great joy which will be for all the people; for today in the city of David there

> has been born for you a Savior, who is Christ the
> Lord. . . . And suddenly there appeared with the
> angel a multitude of the heavenly host praising
> God and saying, "Glory to God in the highest,
> And on earth peace among men with whom He
> is pleased. . . . *But Mary treasured all these things,
> pondering them in her heart.*" (Emphasis added)

Luke records further indication that the birth of Christ was a virgin birth. He stresses that Mary was only "engaged" to be married not married which in those days meant she had not yet had sexual relation with Joseph. The supernatural appearance of the angel and heavenly host points to something amazing that is happening. Mary's reaction and her meditation on the event shows that she knew it was supernatural.

John records in his Gospel some strong intimation that Jesus was virgin–born. At Jesus' first miracle at Cana where Jesus turned water into wine, Mary shows an awareness of His supernatural origin by her confidence that He could do the supernatural given her request (John 2:1–5). This is remarkable given she had never seen Him perform a miracle. She knew of His supernatural origin via His virgin birth. John also records a response by Jesus' enemies that insinuates their awareness of the virgin birth, even though they do not accept it (John 8:41).

The Epistles of the New Testament are filled with references to Jesus' sinlessness, which implies His virgin birth (2 Cor. 5:21; Heb. 4:15; 1 John 3:3). Paul is explicit about it in Galatians 4:4: "But when the fullness of the time came, God sent forth His Son, born of a woman, born under the Law." In the Jewish patriarchal culture, one is begotten of a father (male). So to bring attention to Christ being "born of a woman" is to indicate something unusual—Jesus' virgin birth.

If Jesus of Nazareth was not virgin born, then He inherited a sin nature and is not different than the rest of us. He would need a Savior as well. A drowning person cannot save another person who is drowning. The virgin birth not only was God's way of working around the problem of a sin nature, but made it a "sign" that drew attention to Jesus' supernatural and sinless nature. Hence, the virgin birth is necessary for Jesus' sinless human nature, which was necessary for Him to be "the Lamb of God who takes away the sin of the world!" (John 1:29). Eternal salvation itself is dependent upon the truth of the virgin birth.

Summary

The virgin birth of Christ is anticipation in the Old Testament and is explicit in the New Testament. It was a supernatural sign that Jesus is Immanuel (God with Us). It assured us that He was sinless and through His ministry and miracles in the life of Christ He demonstrates His deity to confirm His message to be the promised Messiah and Son of God who alone could give His sinless life for the sin of the world.

Questions to Answer

1. What biblical verses, from the Old Testament, predict and support the virgin birth of Jesus Christ?
2. What are the main factors that demonstrate the virgin birth in the New Testament?
3. Why is the virgin birth necessary for Jesus to be the sinless (without sin) savior?

3

The Deity of Jesus Christ

*So the Jews said to Him, "You are not yet fifty years old,
and have You seen Abraham?" Jesus said to them, "Tru-
ly, truly, I say to you, before Abraham was born, I am."
Therefore they picked up stones to throw at Him, but
Jesus hid Himself and went out of the temple.*
John 8:57–59

Our study of the Deity of Jesus Christ is demonstrated through His life and ministry on earth, particularly His claims, and teaching about Himself, His miracles and sinlessness life made possible by the virgin birth (Chapter 2). How Jesus can be both human and divine is explored in the study of His incarnation (Chapter 4). An argument for His divinity is found in the Appendix B.

Jesus Christs' Claim to be God

That Jesus Christ is God is affirmed through His life and ministry, both directly and indirectly. Jesus claimed to be Yahweh (Jehovah), He claimed to be equal with God, He claimed to be the Messiah–God, He accepted worship as God, He put His words on par with God's Word. He also accepted prayer in His name, He taught in parables as God, and His disciples acknowledged His claim to be God.

Jesus Claimed to be Yahweh (Jehovah)

Yahweh (YHWH) or Jehovah is the special name for God revealed to Moses in Exodus 3:14. This is the name God gave to Moses when he asked. God said, "I AM WHO I AM." No other person or thing was to receive this name. No one else was to be worshiped or served (Ex. 20:5). Other titles for God may be used for men or even false gods, but not Yahweh. Isaiah wrote, "I am [Yahweh], that is My name; I will not give My glory to another, Nor My praise to graven images" (Isa. 42:8). " 'I am the first and I am the last, And there is no God besides Me' " (Isa. 44:6).

Jesus prayed in John 17:5, "Now, Father, glorify Me together with Yourself, with the glory which I had with You before the world was." This is an obvious claim for Christ's deity. For as we have seen Yahweh does not share His glory (Isa. 42:8). Jesus also declared "I am the first and the last" (Rev. 1:17). Yet these are precisely the words used by Yahweh (Isa. 44:6). Jesus also claimed to be the good shepherd (John 10:11) yet Yahweh is the shepherd (Ps. 23:1). Jesus claimed to be the judge of all men (John 5:27ff; Matt. 25:3ff.) yet Yahweh will judge all the nations (Joel 3:12). Perhaps the strongest claim Jesus made to be Jehovah is in John 8:58: Jesus said to them, "Truly, truly, I say to you, before Abraham was born, I am." In this statement, Jesus claims no only existence before Abraham, but equality with "I AM" of Exodus 3:14. The Jews around Him clearly understood this to be a claim to be Yahweh for they picked up stones to kill Him for blaspheming. Jesus made the same claim in Mark 14:62 and John 18:5–6.

Jesus Claimed to be Equal with God

Jesus also claimed to be equal with God by claiming the prerogatives of God. He told a paralytic that his sins are forgiven (Mark 2:5ff). The scribes correctly responded that only God can forgive sins. Jesus, to prove His claim, healed the man, offering direct proof that what He said about forgiving sins was true. Jesus also claimed the power to raise and judge the dead. Jesus said, "Truly, truly, I say to you, an hour is coming and now is, when the dead will hear the voice of the Son of God, and those who hear will live. . . and will come forth; those who did the good deeds to a resurrection of life, those who committed the evil deeds to a resurrection of judgment" (John 5:25, 29). Yet the Old Testament clearly says that only God is the giver of life (1 Sam. 2:6; Deut. 32:39) and the one to raise the dead (Ps. 2:7) and the only Judge (Joel 3:12; Deut. 32:36). Hence, Jesus does what only God can do.

Jesus Claimed to be the Messiah–God

The Old Testament teaches that the coming Messiah would be God Himself. Isaiah (9:6) calls the Messiah "Mighty God." Likewise the psalmist wrote of the Messiah, "Your throne, O God, is forever and ever." When Jesus claimed to be the Messiah, He was also claiming to be God. Jesus applied the conversation between the Father and the Son in Psalm 110:1 to Himself (Matt. 22:43–44): "The Lord said to my Lord, 'Sit at My right hand.' "

Jesus directly claimed to be the Messiah at His trial before the high priest.

> Again the high priest was questioning Him, and saying to Him, "Are You the Christ, the Son of the Blessed One?" And Jesus said, "I am; and you shall see the Son of Man sitting at the right hand of Power, and coming with the clouds of heaven." Tearing his clothes, the high priest said, "What

further need do we have of witnesses? You have
heard the blasphemy. (Mark 14:61–64)

Jesus Accepted Worship as God

The Old Testament forbids the worship of anyone
other than God (Ex. 20:1–5; Deut. 5:6–9). The New
Testament agrees showing men (Acts 14:13–15) and angels (Rev. 22:8–9) who refused worship. However, Jesus
accepted worship on many occasions which is a claim
to be God. These include the mother of James and John
(Matt. 20:20); the Gerasene demoniac (Mark 5:6); a
healed blind man (John. 9:38); doubting Thomas (John.
20:28); the women at the tomb (Matt. 28:9); a Canaanite
woman (Matt. 15:25); His disciples after the storm (Matt.
14:33); a healed leper (Matt. 8:2); a rich young ruler
(Matt. 9:18) and the disciples at the Great Commission
(Matt. 28:17).

Jesus Put His Words on Par with God's Word

Jesus also put His words on par with God's word. Jesus
frequently said, "You have heard" using a quote from the
Old Testament. Then Jesus says, "But I say to you . . ."
(Matt. 5:21–22). Jesus said, "All authority has been given
to Me in heaven and on earth. Go therefore and make disciples of all the nations" (Matt. 28:18–19). Furthermore,
God gave the Ten Commandments to Moses, But Jesus
said, "A new commandment I give to you, that you love
one another (John 13:34). Jesus promised, "For truly I say
to you, until heaven and earth pass away, not the smallest
letter or stroke shall pass from the Law until all is accomplished" (Matt. 5:18). Jesus expected His words to have
equal authority with God's words in the Old Testament.

Jesus Accepted Prayer as God

Jesus also asked others to pray in His name: "Whatever you ask in My name, that will I do, so that the Father may be glorified in the Son. If you ask Me anything in My name, I will do it" (John 14:13–14). "If you abide in Me, and My words abide in you, ask whatever you wish, and it will be done for you" (John 15:7). Jesus insisted: "no one comes to the Father but through Me" (John 14:6). Clearly Jesus taught that His name be invoked before God and as God in prayer. This is exactly what His disciples did (1 Cor 5:4; Acts 7:59).

Jesus Taught in Parables as God

In the Old Testament God speaks in parables (Ps. 78:1–3). Jesus' teaching in parables depicts Himself as God which is an implicit claim to be God. These images include the Sower, Director of the Harvest, Rock, Shepherd, Bridegroom, Father, Giver of Forgiveness, Vineyard Owner, Lord, and many more.

Any unbiased observer, whether they accept Jesus Christ or not, should recognize that Jesus of Nazareth did claim to be God in the Gospels; that is He unmistakably claimed to be identical to Yahweh (Jehovah) of the Old Testament.

Jesus' Disciples Acknowledged His Claim to be God

Jesus' immediate disciples also acknowledged His claim to deity. They did this in several ways:

1) The disciples attributed the titles of deity to Christ. Some of these include "the first and the last" (Rev. 1:17); "the Chief Shepherd" (1 Peter 5:4); "Redeemer" (Titus 2:13–14); "Forgiver of sins" (Acts 5:31); "Savior of the world" (John 4:42); and "judge" of the living and dead (2 Tim. 4:1).

2) The disciples consider Jesus the Messiah–God. They apply the very title "Christ" to Jesus which has the same meaning of the Hebrew Messiah ("Anointed One"). They call Jesus "Immanuel" ("God with us") from Isa. 7:14. Paul interprets Isaiah 45:22–23 as applying to Jesus "so that at the name of Jesus every knee will bow, of those who are in heaven and on earth and under the earth, and that every tongue will confess that Jesus Christ is Lord" (Phil. 2:10–11).

3) The disciples attributed the power of God to Jesus. They said Jesus is able to raise the dead (John 5:21; 11:38–44); forgive sins (Acts 5:31); be the Creator (John 1:2–3) and sustain existence (Col. 1:17).

4) The disciples associated Jesus' name with God's name. They used His name in prayers and benedictions alongside God's (Gal. 1:3; Eph. 1:2). They place His name on equal status with God's (Matt. 28:19). "The grace of the Lord Jesus Christ, and the love of God, and the fellowship of the Holy Spirit, be with you all" (2 Cor. 13:14).

5) The disciples called Jesus God. Thomas saw His wounds and cried, "My Lord and my God!" (John 20:28). Paul called Jesus "God over all" (Rom. 9:5; cf. Col 2:9). His most direct reference to Jesus Christ being God is found in Phil. 2:5–8 where Jesus Christ is in the "form of a servant" and the "form of God." The parallel phrasing suggests that if Jesus was fully human, then He was fully God. The prologue to John's Gospel directly states: "In the beginning was the Word, and the Word was with God, and the *Word [Jesus] was God*" (John 1:1, emphasis added).

6) The disciples considered Jesus superior to angels. Paul said Jesus was above all other rulers and authorities (Eph. 1:21). Hebrews presents a complete argument for

Christ's superiority over angels. "For to which of the angels did He ever say, 'You are My Son, Today I have begotten You?' " (Heb. 1:5).

So even from those who knew Him best, Jesus, the carpenter of Nazareth, claimed to be God. And was given the titles, powers, prerogatives, and activates that apply only to God. C. S. Lewis, insightfully observed, when confronted with the boldness of Christ's claims, that we are faced with three distinct alternatives:

> I am trying here to prevent anyone saying the really foolish things that people often say about Him: "I'm ready to accept Jesus as a great moral teacher, but I don't accept His claim to be God." That is the one thing we must not say. A man who was merely a man and said the sort of things Jesus said would not be a great moral teacher. He would either be a lunatic—on the level with the man who says he is a poached egg—or else he would be the Devil of Hell. (*Mere Christianity*, 55–56)

The third option is that Jesus was telling the truth: He is Lord. This is established by Jesus in that He not only *claimed* to be God but also *proved* to be God in human flesh by doing miracles and living a sinless live.

THE DEITY OF CHRIST CONFIRMED THROUGH MIRACLES

Christ's Miracles

Jesus did miracles to demonstrate His deity and confirm His message from God. The New Testament records about sixty miracles in the life of Jesus. Indeed, John (20:30) says there were "many other signs Jesus also performed in the presence of the disciples, which are not written in this book; but these have been written so that you may believe that Jesus is the Christ, the Son of God; and that believing you may have life in His name." The purpose of Jesus' miracles can be discovered by examining the terms used to describe them: *sign*, *wonder*, and *power*.

The term "sign" is used forty–eight times in the Gospels. It is used of His most significant miracle, the bodily resurrection of Jesus Christ from the grave. In Matthew 12:39–40, Jesus said:

> An evil and adulterous generation craves for a sign; and yet no sign will be given to it but the *sign* of Jonah the prophet; for just as Jonah was three days and three nights in the belly of the sea monster, so will the Son of Man be three days and three nights in the heart of the earth. (Emphasis added)

Jesus again predicted His resurrection when He was asked for a sign in Matthew 16:1, 4. Hence, the resurrection was clearly something Jesus predicted and accomplished (Matt. 12:39–40; John 2:19; Matt. 16:21; 20:19).

The term "wonder" sometimes translated "miraculous sign" is used sixteen times in the New Testament. It is usually used of a miracle (Acts 2:22) and means something that is amazing or astonishing. Jesus used it of His own miracles in John 4:48: So Jesus said to him, "Unless you people see signs and wonders, you simply will not believe." Peter used it to describe Jesus' miracles in his sermon at Pentecost saying, "Men of Israel, listen to these words: Jesus the Nazarene, a man attested to you by God with miracles and wonders and signs which God performed through Him in your midst, just as you yourselves know" (Acts 2:22).

The term "power" is a generic term used for humans and angels, but is also used of Christ's power to raise the dead (Phil. 3:10) including the miracle of His virgin birth: "The angel answered and said to her, "The Holy Spirit will come upon you, and the power of the Most High will overshadow you; and for that reason the holy Child shall be called the Son of God" (Luke 1:35). The emphasis of the word is on the divine energizing aspect of a miraculous event.

A miracle is a supernatural event (wonder) that has its source in God (power) and its significance (sign) in confirming a message/messenger from God. The purpose of miracles in the New Testament follows that of the Old Testament. They are a divine confirmation of a prophet or spokesperson for God. Moses was told that the purpose of a miracle was so "that they may believe that the Lord, the God of their fathers, the God of Abraham, the God of Isaac, and the God of Jacob, has appeared to you" (Ex. 4:1–5; cf. 1 Kings 18:36).

In the New Testament miracles possess the same confirmatory purpose. John said, "This beginning of His signs Jesus did in Cana of Galilee, and manifested His glory, and His disciples believed in Him" (John 2:11; cf. 20:30–31). Nicodemus said of Jesus: "Rabbi, we know that You have come from God as a teacher; for no one can do these signs that You do unless God is with him." Many followed Jesus because they saw the signs He performed (John 6:2). When some rejected Jesus, even though they had seen His signs they remarked: "How can a man who is a sinner perform such signs?" (John 9:16). Hebrews provides one of the most definitive passages on miracles:

> How will we escape if we neglect so great a salvation? After it was at the first spoken through the Lord, it was confirmed to us by those who heard, God also testifying with them, both by signs and wonders and by various miracles and by gifts of the Holy Spirit according to His own will. (Heb. 2:3–4)

Jesus was known to be from God because of His miracles (John 3:2). Miracles are God's way of accrediting His spokesperson. It confirms the message as true, a sign to substantiate the sermon, an act of God to verify the Word of God (Heb. 2:3–4). Not all believe, even though they witness a miracle (John 12:37). Hence, one result of miracles is the condemnation of the unbeliever (Luke 16:31; John 12:31, 37).

Jesus' Miracles

A miracle is a divine intervention in the natural world that produces an event that would not have resulted from purely natural cause. The primary purpose, but not exclusive purpose, is to confirm a message from God (John 3:2; Acts 2:22; Heb. 2:3). The Gospels record some sixty miracles in the life of Christ. These are clearly miracles because they are immediate (Matt. 8:3), permanent or with no relapses, multiple (Acts 1:3), connected with a truth claim in the name of God (Mark 2:10–11) and contain a predictive element (John 13:19). The following is a list of miracles done by Jesus of Nazareth.

A LIST OF JESUS' RECORDED MIRACLES

Description	Matthew	Mark	Luke	John	Other
Water becomes wine.				2:1–11	
Noble's son healed.				4:46	
Jesus escapes mob.			4:30		
Catch of fish.			5:6		
Unclean spirit cast out.		1:23		4:33	
Peter's mother–in–law healed.	8:14	1:30	4:38		
Sick healed.	8:16	1:32	4:40		
Leper cleansed.	8:2	1:40	5:12		

Description	Matthew	Mark	Luke	John	Other
Paralytic healed.	9:2	2:3	5:18		
Infirm man healed.				5:9	
Withered hand restored.	12:9	3:1	6:6		
Sick healed.	12:15	3:10			
Centurion's servant healed.	8:5	7:1			
Widow's son returned to life.			7:11		
Demon cast from blind mute.	12:22				
Storm stilled.	8:23	4:35	8:22		
Demons cast out and enter herd of swine.	8:28	5:1	8:26		
Ruler's daughter raised.	9:18–23	5:22–35	8:40–49		
Woman with issue of blood healed.	9:20	5:25	8:43		
Blind men healed.	9:27				
Demon cast from deaf mute.	9:32				
Five thousand fed.	14:13	6:30	9:10	6:1	
Jesus walks on sea.	14:25	6:48		6:19	
Sick healed at Gennesaret	14:36	6:56			
Gentile man's daughter healed.	15:21	7:24			
Deaf mute healed.		7:31			
Four thousand fed.	15:32	8:1			
Blind paralytic healed.		8:22			
Jesus' transfiguration.	17:1–8	9:2–8	9:28–36		
Epileptic boy healed.	17:14	9:17	9:38		
Coin in fish's mouth.	17:24				
Man born blind healed.				9:1	
Demon–possessed, blind mute healed.			11:14		
Infirm woman healed.			13:11		
Man with dropsy healed.			14:1–4		
Lazarus raised from dead.				11:43	
Ten lepers cleansed.			17:11		
Two blind men healed.	20:30	10:46	18:35		
Fig tree withers.	21:18	11:12			
Servant's ear restored.			22:51		
Jesus rises from dead.	28	16:1–8	24	20	

Description	Matthew	Mark	Luke	John	Other
Angel rolls stone away, announces resurrection.	28:1–7				
Angel appears at grave.	28:5–8	16:5–7	24:4–8		
Angels appear to Mary.				20:11–13	
Jesus appears to Mary Magdalene.		16:9		20:14–17	
Jesus appears to women.	28:9–10				
Jesus appears on road to Emmaus.		16:12	24:13–35		
Jesus appears to ten.				20:19–23	
Jesus appears to eleven.		16:14–18	24:36–48	20:26–31	
Jesus appears to seven.				21:1–25	
Miraculous catch of fish.				21:6	
Jesus appears to all the apostles.	28:16–20	16:15–18			
Jesus appears to all the apostles.		24:44–53			Acts 1:3–8
Jesus appears to Peter and the apostles					1 Cor. 15:5
Jesus ascends into heaven.					Acts 1:6–9

Jesus Lived a Sinless Life

Jesus was sinless because of His virgin birth (Chapter 1). He challenged others to convict Him of sin by saying, "Which one of you convicts Me of sin?" (John 8:46). His opponents and others said He was righteous. Judas who betrayed him said Jesus was "innocent blood" (Matt. 27:4). Pilate who ultimately condemned Jesus called him "innocent" (Luke 23:14, 15, 26) and a centurion (Luke 23:47). The thief next to Jesus on the cross said He had "done nothing wrong" (Luke 23:41). His supporters and Apostles who were closest to Him acknowledged He was sinless: John the Baptist called Jesus the "the Lamb of God who takes away the sin of the world" (John 1:29). Only a pure lamb could be sacrificed for sin, and only a perfect man could take away the sin of the world. Peter said Jesus "committed no sin" (1 Peter 2:21, 22). The Apostle Paul said Jesus "knew no sin" (2 Cor. 5:21). Hence, Jesus actively lived a life perfectly in accordance with the law and passive obedience to willingly submit to the Father's will in giving His life for the sin of the world.

Summary

Jesus' life and ministry unmistakably involves the direct claim to be God (Yahweh) in the flesh. He accepted worship and prayer as God and placed His words and teaching on par with God. Jesus also did numerous miracles that were immediate, permanent, in the name of God; involve a predictive element and a sinless life. Not only did Jesus have to be sinless to save sinners, He had to be both God and man to be our mediator: "For there is one God, and one mediator also between God and men, the man Christ Jesus" (1 Tim. 2:5).

Questions to Answer

1. What are some of the ways Jesus claimed to be God in the New Testament?
2. How did Jesus' disciples acknowledge He was God?
3. What makes Jesus' miracles unique and genuine?
4. What biblical verses support the sinlessness of Jesus Christ?

4

The Incarnation of Christ

Have this attitude in yourselves which was also in Christ
Jesus, who, although He existed in the form of God, did
not regard equality with God a thing to be grasped, but
emptied Himself, taking the form of a bond–servant, and
being made in the likeness of men.
Philippians 2:5–7

Our study of the Incarnation involves the biblical explanation of the Second Person of the Trinity (see
Appendix A) taking on a permanent human nature.
We then examine the logical validity of the Incarnation.
The incarnation is the theology behind the virgin birth
(Chapter 2) and sinless life of Christ (Chapter 3). It is the
explanation of how God became man, so that He might
willingly lay down His life on the cross and rise from the
dead (Chapter 5) so that He might be the atoning substitute for sin (Chapter 6).

Jesus Christ's Incarnation

Jesus Christ's incarnation (Latin for *in* and *carn*, meaning "flesh") is implicit in His claim to be the promised Jewish Messiah and God. Jesus taught this truth to His disciples and argued for it with His enemies. In Matthew 16:15–17 Jesus posed the question to Peter and the disciples, "But who do you say that I am?" The accepted answer is "You are the Christ, the Son of the living God." And the source of this answer was from God the Father. In Matthew 22:41–46 Jesus possess the question to the Pharisees, What do you think about the Christ, whose son is He? The answer was "The Son of David." To prove this, Jesus quoted the Psalm of David (110) putting them in a dilemma: How can He be the son of David and also be David's Lord? The only answer to the question that escapes the dilemma is that Jesus was both God and man, or God incarnate.

A biblical argument for Jesus' deity can be made as follows: 1) God is the only savior. Isaiah 43:11 says "I, even I, am the LORD, and apart from me there is no savior." 2) Jesus is the savior. Luke 2:11 says "Today in the town of David a Savior has been born to you; he is Christ the Lord." 3) Therefore, Jesus is God as Paul calls Jesus, the "Savior . . . the Lord Jesus Christ" (Phil. 3:20).

Jesus Christ is Fully God and Fully Human

Jesus is presented in the New Testament as being fully human. He has a human genealogy (Matt. 1:1–17), born of a woman (Matt. 1:18f; Gal. 4:4), He aged (Luke 2:42), increased in knowledge, (Matt. 4:12), prayed (Matt. 14:23), grew hungry (Matt. 4:2), tired (John 4:6), had compassion (Matt. 9:36), wept (John 11:35), grew thirsty (John 19:28) and Jesus is referred to as the "Son of Man" and "Son of David" multiple times. Jesus said,

"Foxes have holes and birds of the air have nests, but the Son of Man has no place to lay his head" (Matt. 8:20).

Jesus is likewise presented in the New Testament as being fully God. He is the Creator (John 1:1–3) and sustainer of creation (1 Cor. 8:6). He is Eternal (John 8:58) "I tell you the truth," Jesus answered, "Before Abraham was born, I am!" Which is a clear reference to the Yahweh of the Old Testament (Ex.3:14). In John 17:5 Jesus says, "And now, Father, glorify me in your presence with the glory I had with you before the world began." Jesus is present everywhere (omnipresence) saying, "Go therefore and make disciples of all the nations . . . Teaching them to obey everything I have commanded you. And surely I am with you always, to the very end of the age" (Matt. 28:20). Jesus is all–knowing (omniscience) "He did not need man's testimony about man, for he knew what was in a man" (John 2:25). But Scripture teaches that only God knows what is in a man's heart (1 Kings 8:39). Jesus is all–powerful (omnipotence) "Then Jesus came to them and said, 'All authority in heaven and on earth has been given to me'" (Matt. 28:18). Jesus is unchangeable (Immutable), "Jesus Christ is the same yesterday and today and forever (Heb. 13:8). Jesus performs the works of God as Judge (John 5:21–27) and power to do miracles such as raising the dead (John 11:43). But as we have seen only God can be and do all of these. Hence, Jesus must be fully God.

The Hypostatic Union

Theologically the incarnation is described as a hypostatic union. A *hypostasis* is a complete individual substance and called a *person* if it has intellect and will. The hypostasis of the second person of the Trinity is said to subsist or cohere in two natures, one divine and one human without mixture, separation, or division. Therefore, Christ can be said to be truly God and truly man: The God–Man. The effecting of this union did not alter the divine nature in any way; both natures retain that which makes them what they are. The human nature being created, limited, and changing is like ours in all respects, except, even though undergoing real temptation, is without sin.

The divine nature being the Second Person of the Trinity (i.e., Divine Logos) took on Himself humanity, but not in a different person or man. Before His conception, He did not possess humanity permanently. He is, since His conception, clothed in humanity forever more. This means that the Second Person of the Trinity, God the Son while in and united to the human body of Jesus is not bound by the human nature assumed.

The person of Christ is held to subsist or cohere in two natures, one divine and one human. Explained in the Trinity, this is two "What's" in one "Who"; two objects in one subject, two essences or natures in one person; two sources of objective coherence subsisting in a single subjective center of volitional and intentional activity (Figure 4.1). These natures are united in one person (hypostatic union), not two persons. The two natures of Christ are conjoined within the one person without mixture, separation, or division. The effecting of this union did not alter the divine nature in any way; both natures retain that which makes them what they are. Therefore, Christ can be said to be truly God and truly man: The God–Man.

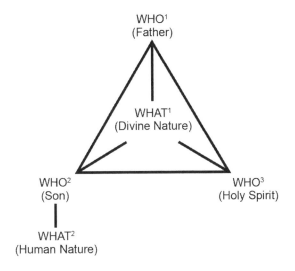

WHO¹
(Father)

WHAT¹
(Divine Nature)

WHO²
(Son)

WHO³
(Holy Spirit)

WHAT²
(Human Nature)

Figure 4.1

Because of the uniqueness of the incarnation, in speaking or answering questions about Jesus it is necessary to ask and answer any question according to each distinct nature. For example, we might ask did Jesus grow tired. We must answer according to each nature, as man (human nature) yes, as God (divine nature) no. Does Jesus know everything? As man no, as God yes. This helps explain why Jesus did know some things that only God knows, such as what was in a man (John 2:25) and did not know other things, that only the Father knows such as the day of His coming (Matt. 24:36). The human nature of Christ grows, learns, and changes over time. It is the divine nature that is immutable (unchanging), knows all, and is eternal. In Figure 4.2 the triangle is the divine nature that is unlimited and never changes and the circle is the human nature of Christ that is limited and changes.

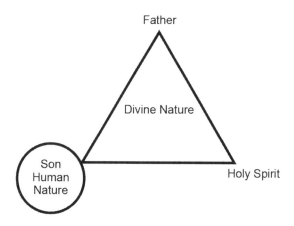

Figure 5.2 Christ's Divine & Human Nature

Figure 4.2

This distinction also helps answer some questions. While all agree that Jesus did not sin, could Jesus have sinned? The answer is as man, yes, as God no. This enables us to see that His temptation to sin was as real as ours (Heb. 4:15), yet His divine nature ensures that He is sinless, and therefore can be our sinless substitute on the cross (1 Peter 1:24). Also the question as to how many "wills" did Jesus have is answerable. He had two, one human will and the divine will. Hence, He can pray to the Father, "Your will be done" (Matt. 26:42).

THE LOGIC OF THE INCARNATION

Some object saying that it is contradictory to affirm that Christ is both infinite (fully God) and finite (fully man) in His being at the same time? However, to be contradictory, one must show that we are affirming "A" and its opposite "non–A" at the same time and in the same sense. The solution is the teaching of the Trinity. The Second Person of the Trinity or the Divine Logos took on Himself humanity, not another person or already existing man. He did not possess humanity before His conception. He is, since His conception clothed in humanity forever more. This means that the Second Person of the Trinity, God the Son while in and united to the human body of Jesus is not bound by the human nature assumed (see Phil. 2:7–8 ; John 1:14; Rom. 1:3; 8:3; Gal. 4:4; 1 Tim. 3:16; 1 John 4:2, 2 John 7). The person of Christ is held to subsist or cohere in two natures, one divine and one human. That is, there are now two "Whats" in one "Who" two objects in one subject, two essences or natures in one Person (Figure 4.1).

It is true that Christianity affirms that Christ is both infinite and finite at the same time. However, it does not maintain that Christ is both infinite and finite in the same sense (If it did it would be contradiction). The orthodox position is that Christ is both infinite in one nature and finite in another nature at the same time, but not in the same sense. Infinitude and finitude are predicated of two different natures united in one person without mixture, confusion or division. Hence, no contradiction is involved.

Only the Athanasius view in the early church preserved the orthodox understanding the Deity and humanity of Jesus Christ. The heretical views that deny or diminish the deity of the Lord are Arianism–denied His deity and held He was created, Adoptionism–Jesus was adopted as a son because of His divine powers, and Subordinationism–the Son is subordinate in nature to the Father. Those that deny or diminish the humanity of the Lord are Docetism–Jesus only appeared to be human and Apollinariansim–diminished His humanity by saying

He had no human spirit. Those that separate the divine
and human relations are Nestorianism–held there were
two persons in Christ and Modalism (or Sabellianism)–
held only one person who appears in different modes.
Eutychanism (or Monophysitism) merged or confused
the two natures which is contradictory (Table 4.1).

	DEITY	HUMANITY	RELATION
Athanasian Creed (Orthodxy)	Affirmed	Affirmed	United
Arianism	Denied	Affirmed	United
Adoptionism	Denied	Affirmed	Adopted
Subordinationism	Diminished	Affirmed	United
Docetism	Affirmed	Denied	Merged
Apollinarianism	Affirmed	Diminished	United
Nestorianism	Affirmed	Affirmed	Separated*
Modalism (Sabellianism)	Affirmed	Affirmed	Separated*
Eutychianism (Monophysitism)	Affirmed	Affirmed	Merged

*Nestorians have three persons in the Trinity, but Modalists have only one.
Nestorians have two separated persons in the Son, one in each nature,
while Modalists have only one person in God, who is performing three
roles.

Table 4.1

SUMMARY

Jesus Christ is the second person of the Trinity who took
on a permanent human nature; such that He remained
fully God and fully man, without mixture, confusion, or
division. Christ is a complete Person, or hypostasis, being one "Who" with no logical contradiction between His
two natures or "Whats," human and divine. As such, His
death on the cross and resurrection (Chapter 5) fully provides for the salvation through His substitutionary atonement (Chapter 6).

Questions to Answer

1. What biblical evidence supports the full humanity and deity of Jesus Christ?
2. What does the hypostatic union of Jesus Christ entail?
3. Why is it important to keep the human and divine natures of Christ distinct?
4. How is the incarnation of Jesus not a logical contradiction?
5. What is the correct or orthodox view regarding the incarnation of Jesus Christ?

5

The Death and Resurrection of Christ

Men of Israel, listen to these words: Jesus the Nazarene,
a man attested to you by God with miracles and wonders
and signs which God performed through Him in your
midst, just as you yourselves know— this Man, delivered
over by the predetermined plan and foreknowledge of
God, you nailed to a cross by the hands of godless men
and put Him to death. But God raised Him up again,
putting an end to the agony of death, since it was impos-
sible for Him to be held in its power.
Acts 2:22–24

Our study of the death and resurrection of Christ begins with His status as a Prophet, Priest, and King which clearly makes His death vicarious or substitutionary. We then cover the descriptions and evidence of Christ's physical death and resurrection.

Christ as Prophet, Priest and King

His death is vicarious or substitutionary because Jesus Christ is a Prophet predicted to come by Moses: "I will raise up a prophet from among their countrymen like you, and I will put My words in his mouth, and he shall speak to them all that I command him" (Deut. 18:18). The New Testament applies what Moses said here to Christ (Acts 7:37). Jesus' teachings recorded in the Gospels were part of His prophetic ministry.

Jesus not only came to speak as a prophet, but also to be a sacrifice. Christ is a Priest, who alone is a mediator between man and God and able to lay down His life. Jesus said, "For even the Son of Man did not come to be served, but to serve, and to give His life a ransom for many" (Mark 10:45). Hence, Jesus' death was not merely exemplar, but it was also sacrificial. He died in our place as a substitute for our sines (Isa. 53:4–7; 2 Cor. 5:21), see Chapter 6.

Christ is also King. One day Jesus will literally be King over His people. He said, "Truly I say to you, that you who have followed Me, in the regeneration when the Son of Man will sit on His glorious throne, you also shall sit upon twelve thrones, judging the twelve tribes of Israel" (Matt. 19:28). Indeed, Christ is called "KING OF KINGS AND LORD OF LORDS" (Rev. 19:16; cf. 20:4–6).

CHRIST'S PHYSICAL DEATH

Christ's resurrection is predicted in the Old Testament in two central passages. Psalm 2:7 says, "I will surely tell of the decree of the Lord: He said to Me, 'You are My Son, Today I have begotten You.'" This is applied to Jesus' resurrection in Acts 13:33–34 (cf. Heb. 1:5):

> that God has fulfilled this promise to our children in that He raised up Jesus, as it is also written in the second Psalm, 'You are My Son; today I have begotten You.' As for the fact that He raised Him up from the dead, no longer to return to decay, He has spoken in this way: 'I will give you the holy and sure blessings of David.'

Psalm 16:10 affirms "For You will not abandon my soul to Sheol; Nor will You allow Your Holy One to undergo decay." Peter argues in Acts 2:29–32 that this must refer to Christ:

> Brethren, I may confidently say to you regarding the patriarch David that he both died and was buried, and his tomb is with us to this day. And so, because he was a prophet and knew that God had sworn to him with an oath to seat one of his descendants on his throne, he looked ahead and spoke of the resurrection of the Christ, that He was neither abandoned to Hades, nor did His flesh suffer decay. This Jesus God raised up again, to which we are all witnesses.

The concept of the resurrection being in the flesh is also present in the Old Testament. Job 19:25–26 (cf. Acts 2) says, "As for me, I know that my Redeemer lives, and at the last He will take His stand on the earth. Even after my skin is destroyed, yet from my flesh I shall see God."

Jesus predicted His own resurrection early in His ministry (John 2:19–22) and later in His ministry (Matt. 12:39:40). These became more frequent and specific, Matthew 17:22–23 says, "And while they were gathering together in Galilee, Jesus said to them, 'The Son of Man is going to be delivered into the hands of men; and they will kill Him, and He will be raised on the third day.' And they were deeply grieved" (cf. John 10:18).

Christ's Physical Death

That Jesus physically died on the cross is well established. Evidence is found in the Bible and outside sources. The Old Testament predicted the Messiah would die (Isa. 53:5–10; Ps. 22:16; Dan. 9:26; Zech. 12:10). Jesus also predicted His death and resurrection (John 2:19–21;

10:10–11; Matt. 12:40; 17:22–23; Mark 8:31). This is important since only a dead body can be resurrected.

Christ's death consisted of passion culminated in the crucifixion to ensure His death. It begins with no sleep the night before He was crucified. He was beaten several times and whipped (shredding His back). He collapsed on His way to the execution site carrying His cross. This alone was totally exhausting and life draining.

The nature of the crucifixion assures death. Jesus was on the cross from 9:00 AM to just before sunset (Mark 15:25, 33). He bled from wounded hands and feet and also from a crown of thorns that pierced His head. The loss of blood plus the demand that He constantly pull Himself up in order to breathe, would cause excruciating pain from the nails.

Jesus' side was pierced with a spear and "blood and water" (John 19:34) came out which is proof that He had physically died before He was pierced. When this happened it is a medical fact that the person has already expired.

Just before He died on the cross Jesus declared, "Father, into Your hands I commit My spirit. Having said this, He breathed His last" (Luke 23:46). Those who remained heard this.

Roman soldiers, accustomed to crucifixion and death, pronounced Jesus dead. It was common to break the legs of the victim to speed death; however they did not do so with Jesus because He was already dead (John 19:33 cf. Ps. 34:20).

Pilate double–checked to make sure Jesus was dead before giving up His corpse to Joseph of Arimathea. "Pilate wondered if He was dead by this time, and summoning the centurion, he questioned him as to whether He was already dead. And ascertaining this from the centurion, he granted the body to Joseph" (Mark 15:44–45).

"Nicodemus . . . also came, bringing a mixture of myrrh and aloes, about hundred pounds. So they took the body of Jesus and bound it in linen wrappings with the spices, as is the burial custom of the Jews" (John 19:39–40). Jesus was placed in a sealed tomb for three days. If He was not dead before that (and He clearly was) He would have died from a lack of food, water and medical treatment.

Modern medical authorities have investigated the circumstances and nature of Jesus' death and have published their conclusions in journals such as the *Journal of the American Medical Society*. They concluded Jesus actually died on the cross.

> Clearly, the weight of historical and medical evidence indicates that Jesus was dead before the wound to his side was inflicted and supports the traditional view that the spear, thrust between his right ribs, probably perforated not only the right lung but also the pericardium and heart thereby ensured his death. Accordingly, interpretations based on the assumption that Jesus did not die on the cross appear to be at odds with modern medical knowledge (*Journal of the American Medical Association* [Mar. 21, 1986]: 1463).

Ancient non–Christian historians and writers from the first and second centuries recorded the death of Christ. These include the Jewish historian of the time of Christ, Flavious Josephus (c. 37–100), the Roman historian Cornelius Tacitus (c. 55–117), the first–century Samaritan Thallus (c. A.D. 52) as recorded by Julius Africanus (c. A.D. 211), the second–century Greek writer Lucian (2nd Century Greek writer) and the Roman writer Phlegon. Even the Babylonian Talmud mentions the hanging death of Yeshu (Jesus).

Early Christian writers, such as Polycarp, Ignatius, Origin, and Justin Martyr, also affirmed Jesus' death and some even cited non–Christian writers mentioning Jesus' death.

The testimony is unbroken: from the Old Testament to the early church Fathers, including believers and unbelievers, Jews and Gentiles. The evidence is overwhelming that Jesus really suffered and died on the cross. The death of Christ by crucifixion is a historical fact beyond all reasonable doubt.

Christ's Physical Resurrection from the Dead

Given Jesus' true death on the cross, the evidence that He actually raised from the dead consists of the empty tomb and His numerous appearances.

Direct Evidence

There are direct and indirect evidence for the resurrection of Christ. The direct evidence includes the empty tomb and the resurrection appearances. They must be considered together, since by themselves they do not constitute proof that the body that died had indeed been raised. (John 2:19).

All the Gospels mentioned the empty tomb (Matt. 28:1–8; Mark 16:1–8; Luke 24:1–12; John 20:1–8). In each case they see His vacated tomb with an angel to confirm that "He is not here. He is risen" (Matt. 28:6; Mark 16:6; Luke 24:6; John 20:12). John mentions the empty grave clothes with the headcloth folded up in a place by itself. This alone, was evidence enough to convince John that Jesus had risen (John 20:6–8).

In the first century Jewish culture, a woman's testimony was not considered valid in a court. Hence, it is a sign of authenticity that Jesus first appeared to women. He appeared to Mary Magdalene (John 10:1–18). She *saw* Jesus standing there (v. 14). She *heard* Jesus say her name and speak to her (v. 15–16). She *touched* Jesus' resurrected body (v. 17). The same word for *touching* is used of Christ's per–resurrection body (Mark 6:56; Luke 6:19). She also witnessed the empty tomb and saw that the stone had been removed from the entrance (v. 2). The parallel account in Matthew 28:6 adds that she was invited by the angel to see the place where He was lying. Having all these human senses used is significant support for the physical nature of the resurrection. Hearing alone is not sufficient to demonstrate materiality, since God is immaterial, yet His voice was heard. But all the evidence together is unmistakable identity of the same, physical body that was raised immortal is present in this first appearance.

He appeared also to the other women with Mary Magdalene (Matthew 28:1–10). This includes Mary the mother of James and Salome (Mark 16:1). Likewise they witnessed the empty tomb (v. 6). They also *saw* and *heard* and *touched* (v. 9) His physical body that came out of the tomb. Matthew 28:9 says, "And behold, Jesus met them and greeted them. And they came up and took hold of His feet and worshiped Him." Again, all four evidences (empty tomb, seeing, hearing, and touching the risen Christ) show the visible, material resurrection of the same (numerically identical) body were present.

Jesus appeared to Peter (1 Cor. 15:5; cf. John 20:3–9) and was seen and likely heard him. Peter also previously saw the empty tomb and grave cloths (John 20:6–7).

Peter experienced all four of the evidences of the physical resurrection (empty tomb, seeing, hearing, and touching the risen Christ).

Jesus appeared to two disciples on the road to Emmaus (Luke 24:13–35; Mark 16:12–13), they saw, heard and ate with Jesus. Here three evidences of the resurrection are presented. One disciple was named Cleopas (v. 18). At first they did not recognize who He was, but then clearly saw Him. When they realized who it was, the text says, "He vanished from their sight" (v. 31). This entails that He was as visible as any other material object. They heard His teaching with their ears (vv. 17, 19, 25–26). A further evidence of Jesus' physical resurrection was that He ate with the two disciples. Later in the chapter it explicitly states that Jesus ate with the ten apostles (v. 43). Luke also states in two other places that Jesus ate with the disciples (Acts 1:4; 10:41). It is hard to imagine any better demonstration of the genuine physical nature of the resurrection body.

Jesus appeared to ten disciples (Luke 24:36–49; John 20:19–23), with Thomas being absent, and Jesus was *seen*, *heard* and He showed them His wounds also implying that He was *touched*. He further *ate* physical food to convince the disciples that He was raised in a literal, physical body. It may be inferred from this occasion that they at first were unconvinced of His tangible materiality. Jesus presented His wounds to them. In fact, Jesus said "See My hands and My feet, that it is I Myself; touch Me and see, for a spirit does not have flesh and bones as you see that I have" (v. 39). Jesus use of "I" and "me" clearly indicates the same (numerically) identical connection with His pre–resurrection body. To further convince them Jesus *ate* physical food. Jesus said, " 'Have you anything here to eat?' They gave Him a piece of a broiled fish; and He took it and ate it before them." Hence, Jesus offered His ability to eat physical food as a demonstration of the material nature of His body of flesh and bones.

A week later, Jesus appeared to eleven disciples (John 20:24–31), with Thomas being present. Thomas refused to believe unless he could see and handle Christ for himself. A week later, his wish was granted (v. 26). There Thomas saw His crucifixion wounds, heard, and likely touched Jesus. That fact that Jesus still had these physical wounds from His crucifixion is an unmistakable proof that He was resurrected in the very same material body in which He was crucified.

Jesus appeared to seven disciples (John 21) who went fishing in Galilee. They saw, heard and ate breakfast with Jesus further demonstrating His tangible, physical nature of His resurrection body; emphasizing Jesus' real activity in space and time. He was seen early in the morning standing on the shore (v. 4). Jesus carried on an extended conversation with Peter (vv. 15–17). Although the text is not explicit that Jesus ate; it nevertheless shows that He was the host of the meal (vv. 10–13), making it quite strange if He did not partake with them.

Jesus appeared to all the Apostles at the giving of the Great Commission (Matt. 28:16–20; Mark 16:14–18). Here Jesus is seen and worshiped (vv. 16–17). Mark adds that they were eating (Mark 16:24). Luke adds that Jesus spoke about the kingdom of God (Acts 1:3) and commanded them (Acts 1:4). This implies a familiarity with His voice and teaching which the apostles heard from the very same Jesus before and after the resurrection. Luke records that Jesus ate with the disciples (Acts 1:4). The intimate fellowship and physical ability to eat food provided sufficient proof that Jesus appeared to them in the same physical body He possessed before His resurrection.

That last appearance of Jesus was to Paul after the Ascension (1 Cor. 15:8; Acts 9:1–9). Paul called this an "appearance" which confirmed him as an Apostle (Acts 1:22; cf. 1 Cor. 9:1). This reference is important because Paul had "visions" (Acts 26:19) but never referred to Jesus' resurrection as a "visions." Paul saw and heard Jesus which is always indicative of a true physical appearance rather than a mere vision. Those who were with Paul saw and heard the voice which shows the experience was not private. Hence, the evidence for the physical resurrection of Christ is overwhelming (Table 5.1).

THE TWELVE APPEARANCES OF CHRIST				
Person	**Saw**	**Hear**	**Touched**	**Comments**
Mary (John 20:10–18)	●	●	●	Empty Tomb
Mary & women (Matt. 28:1–10)	●	●	●	Empty Tomb
Peter & John (1 Cor. 15:5; Jn, 20:1–10)	●	●*		Empty Tomb, grave cloths
Two disciples (Luke 24:13–35)	●	●		Ate food
Ten Apostles (Lk, 24:36–49; John 20:19–23)	●	●	●†	Death wounds, ate food
Eleven Apostles (John 20:24–31)	●	●	●†	Death wounds
Seven Apostles (John 21)	●	●		Ate food
All Apostles (Matt. 28:16–20; Mark 16:14–18)	●	●		
500 Brethren (1Cor, 15:6)	●	●*		
James (1 Cor. 15:7)	●	●*		
All Apostles (Acts 1:4–8)	●	●		Ate food
Paul (Acts 9:1–9; 1 Cor. 15:8)	●	●		

*Implied, †Offered to be touched

Table 5.1

Jesus was seen by more than five hundred people over a forty–day period of time and on twelve occasions Jesus was not only seen, but heard. For times He offered himself to be touched and He was definitely touched twice.

Jesus revealed His crucifixion scars on two occasions and atc food on four occasions. Add to this the four times the empty tomb was seen and twice the empty grave clothes were viewed. The sum total of this evidence is tremendous confirmation that Jesus rose and lived in the same visible, material body He possessed before His resurrection.

Indirect Evidence

In addition to direct evidence of Jesus bodily resurrection, there is indirect confirming evidence. These begin with the immediate transformation of the disciples. After Jesus' death His disciples were scared, scattered, and skeptical about reports of Jesus' resurrection (Luke 24:11). The apostles doubted the report of the women who first saw the empty tomb and the risen Christ. Some doubted until they saw Christ for themselves. Yet within a few weeks these same skeptical disciples, (John 20:19) were fearless and openly proclaiming the resurrection of Jesus in the face of death (Acts 4–5). The best explanation for this is the bodily resurrection of Christ.

It is worth noting the central focus of apostolic preaching. Of all the things Jesus taught about such as love, non–retaliation and the Kingdom of God, the central focus of apostolic preaching was the resurrection of Jesus Christ. Acts 4:33 says "And with great power the Apostles were giving testimony to the resurrection of the Lord Jesus, and abundant grace was upon them all." Such emphasis is found throughout the book of Acts (Acts 2:22ff.; 3:15, 25; 4:33) The best explanation of this is repeated encounters of Jesus alive after His crucifixion.

The reaction of those who rejected Christ provides testimony to the fact of the resurrection. They did not *refute* it, rather, they *resisted* it (Acts 4:2ff). Surely if they could have found Jesus' body, they would have produced it and defeated the claim of His disciples. Instead of *finding* the dead body, they *fought* the disciples who testified to Him being alive. They persecuted the witnesses of the resurrection, instead of disproving them. This is certainly evidence that what the disciples witnessed was real. The authorities could only discredit the resurrection by bribing the guards (Matt. 28:11ff.). The claim that Jesus' body was stolen shows the desperate attempt to resist the reality of the resurrection.

Another proof of the resurrection is the very existence of the early church. There are several reasons the church should not have arisen. The original church consisted mostly of Jews who believed in only one God (Deut. 6:4). This makes it very unlikely that they would accept Jesus as God. But they prayed to Jesus (Acts 7:59), exalted Him to the right hand of God (Acts 2:33) and called Him Lord and Christ (Acts 2:34–36) which were the very titles that brought the charge of blasphemy from the Jewish high priest. Furthermore, the first Christians were persecuted, beaten, threatened with death and martyred (Acts 7:57–60). Under these conditions, they maintained their belief (which could have been given up, *but was not*) and increased in numbers daily. Only an encounter with the resurrected Christ can account for this Jewish sect that later came to be known as "Christians" (Acts 11:26).

Christianity experienced an immediate and rapid growth. Three thousand were saved the very first day (Acts 2:41). Many were added to their ranks daily (Acts 2:47). Within days five thousand more became believers (Acts 4:4). Add to this the rapid nature of their growth (Acts 4:4, 6:1).

The first–century priests were the guardians of Jewish religious beliefs and traditions. They were in constant conflict with Jesus and His followers. Yet soon after Jesus' resurrection many Jewish priests who had access to the evidence and a strong motive not to convert became believers (Acts 6:7).

The least likely to be converted was Saul of Tarsus, a well–educated Pharisee who persecuted Christians (Acts 9:1). He was one of the most zealous anti–Christians of the day (Phil. 3:4–6). Nothing short of a real encounter with the resurrected Christ can account for all this (Acts 9).

Taken together, the evidence for the resurrection of Christ is voluminous and compelling. There is nothing like it for any other historical event from the ancient world. The amount of direct and indirect evidence presents an overwhelming case for the physical resurrection of Christ "beyond all reasonable doubt."

Some have tried to show that Paul's teaching seems to indicate that the resurrection body is spiritual or immaterial. For Paul says, "it is raised a spiritual body. If there is a natural body, there is also a spiritual body" (1 Cor. 15:44) and "that flesh and blood cannot inherit the kingdom of God. . . ." (50–51). However, the use of the term "spiritual" Paul uses can be translated "supernatural" and Paul uses this of a physical "rock" too (1 Cor. 10:4). So Paul is using "spiritual body" to denote the immortal body (not one devoid of matter). It is not used for immaterial and invisible, but immortal and imperishable. It is to designate a body directed by the Spirit of God as opposed to the flesh. When Paul says "flesh and bones" cannot inherit the kingdom of God, it is to designate "perishable" flesh and bones that is mortal. Paul clarifies this by saying, "nor does the perishable inherit the imperishable" (1 Cor. 15:50). We know Jesus' resurrected body was "flesh and bones" (Luke 24:39) and our resurrection bodies will be like His (1 John 3:2).

Summary

Jesus Christ perfectly fulfills the role of Prophet, Priest, and King. His death on the cross is substitutionary. His death and resurrection is predicted in the Old Testament. His physical death is well established in Scripture, history, and by modern medical analysis. His physical resurrection is demonstrated through the direct evidence of His empty tomb and numerous resurrection appearances. The indirect evidence is demonstrated through the transformation of the disciples who are responsible for the birth of the Church.

Questions to Answer

1. How is Jesus a Prophet, Priest, and King?
2. What evidence supports the physical death of Jesus Christ?
3. What evidence supports the physical resurrection of Jesus?
4. What do the resurrection appearances of Jesus Christ tell us about the nature of the resurrection body?
5. How do the lives and testimony of the apostles support the truth of the resurrection of Jesus?

6

The Atonement, Assumption & Present Session of Christ

My little children, I am writing these things to you so that you may not sin. And if anyone sins, we have an Advocate with the Father, Jesus Christ the righteous; and He Himself is the propitiation for our sins; and not for ours only, but also for those of the whole world.
1 John 1:1–2

Our study of the atonement begins by examining the substitutionary nature of salvation. We then explore Christ's bodily assumption and present session.

The Substitutionary Atonement of Christ

The Old Testament Hebrew word for *atonement* is used about 100 times and carries the meaning "to cover, expiate, wipe away, placate, or cancel." It is used to indicate a covering over in God's eyes or a wiping away. The New Testament word for *atonement* means "to propitiate, expiate, or conciliate." Hebrews 2:17 says, "Therefore, He had to be made like His brethren in all things, so that He might become a merciful and faithful high priest in things pertaining to God, *to make propitiation* [atonement] for the sins of the people" (emphasis added).

Christ's atonement at the cross is evident in the Old Testament sacrificial system. The blood atonement of spotless innocent animals was regularly required for sins (Lev. 4:14–21). The Scriptures teach that blood is necessary for atonement. Leviticus 17:11 says, "For the life of the flesh is in the blood, and I have given it to you on the altar to make atonement for your souls; for it is the blood by reason of the life that makes atonement." This pointed forward to Christ's once–for–all blood sacrifice for human sins (1 Cor. 5:7). Hebrews 9:22 adds, "And according to the Law, one may almost say, all things are cleansed with blood, and without shedding of blood there is no forgiveness." Hence, this points to the necessity of Christ's blood sacrifice on the cross for the remission of sins. Nothing but the blood sacrifice of Jesus, who is the Lamb of God, could take away the sins of all humankind (John 1:29).

Scripture indicates that Christ's atonement is substitutionary. Christ died in our place. He was punished for our sins that we might be set free. While there are other views on the atonement, there are many biblical reasons to accept His atonement in this way.

The necessity of a substitutionary atonement is grounded in God's absolute justice that demands a perfect substitute for our sins because they cannot be overlooked (Hab. 1:13). God is essentially just and cannot be otherwise.

It is seen in total depravity in that it demands a perfect substitute for sins, since we cannot measure up to God's holiness. There is nothing humans can do to measure up to God's perfect standard. Only a substitutionary sacrifice can rectify this human dilemma.

The Old Testament foresaw this and pictured it in the animal sacrifices implying a substitutionary atonement when hands were laid on an animal to symbolize the transfer of guilt (Lev. 1:3–4).

Isaiah 53:5–6 is explicit about substitutionary atonement:

> But He was pierced through for our transgressions,
> He was crushed for our iniquities;
> The chastening for our well–being fell upon Him,
> And by His scourging we are healed.
> All of us like sheep have gone astray,
> Each of us has turned to his own way;
> But the Lord has caused the iniquity of us all
> To fall on Him.

Jesus also claimed to be the fulfillment of Isaiah 53 which is clearly substitutionary (Luke 22:37).

Jesus Christ was presented as the Passover lamb. John the Baptist declared "Behold, the Lamb of God who takes away the sin of the world!" (John 1:29) and the apostle Paul said, "Christ our Passover also has been sacrificed (1 Cor. 5:7).

Jesus also presented His death as a ransom, payment or offering as a substitute. Mark 10:45 says, "For even the Son of Man did not come to be served, but to serve, and to give His life a ransom for many."

Jesus presented himself as a consecrated Priest and sacrifice (John 17:19). Hebrews 9:7, 15 says,

> Only the high priest enters once a year, not without taking blood, which he offers for himself and for the sins of the people committed in ignorance. . . . For this reason He is the mediator of a new covenant, so that, since a death has taken place for the redemption of the transgressions

that were committed under the first covenant, those who have been called may receive the promise of the eternal inheritance.

Hebrews goes on to teach that Christ said to the Father, "Sacrifice and offering You have not desired, But a body You have prepared for Me" (Heb. 10:5) and Jesus died on our behalf "By this will we have been sanctified through the offering of the body of Jesus Christ once for all" (Heb. 10:10).

Furthermore, Christ's death was "for" another which implies substitution (Luke 22:19–20; John 10:15; Rom. 5:8; Gal. 3:13) and his death was "for" an explicit substitution (Matt. 20:28). The word *expiation* is used of Christ's death that implies substitutionary sacrifice 1 John 2:2 says, "He Himself is the propitiation for our sins; and not for ours only, but also for those of the whole world."

Many times the New Testament speaks of the wrath of God against sin (Rom. 1:18; 2:5, 8' 5:9; 9:22; 12:19; 13:4–5). This necessitates Christ's substitutionary sacrifice. The only way to appease God's wrath is by Christ's death which implies a substitutionary death (Rom. 3:25).

Indeed, the Apostle Paul teaches:

Christ died for our sins according to the Scriptures (1 Cor. 15:3).

He made Him who knew no sin to be sin on our behalf, so that we might become the righteousness of God in Him (2 Cor 5:21).

For Christ also died for sins once for all, the just for the unjust, so that He might bring us to God (1 Peter 3:18).

Some object that it was unfair for God to punish Jesus Christ for our sins (John 10:17–18). But Christ is

God (Chapter 5); so the one who demanded the penalty (God) was the One who willingly paid it. God's justice demands that all sin be punished, but not necessarily that all sinners be punished for their sin. Furthermore, mercy triumphs justice. God's justice demands punishment of the sinner, but the Cross (His love) wins out. The obligation to what is always wrong, not to punish the guilty, is suspended in view of the higher obligation to what is always right, to save the repentant sinner.

Some object saying righteousness cannot be transferred to another. However, it is possible for it to be imputed legally or judiciously to those who believe because they are united to Christ. We are righteous in Christ, not ourselves (2 Cor. 5:17).

Some object saying the sacrifice of Christ was not necessary, that God could forgive sins without it. However, our ability to forgive is based on Christ's forgiveness. No mortal has the inherent ability to forgive (Mark 2:7). God is absolutely just by nature and cannot overlook sin (Hab. 1:13). He cannot overlook or accept sin since it causes a debt that can no more be overlooked than He can change His nature. And since God made a covenant (Heb. 9:16, 22) that demands the shedding of blood for the forgiveness of sins, then the sacrifice of Christ is necessary for the forgiveness for salvation.

CHRIST'S BODILY ASSUMPTION AND PRESENT SESSION

The primary text on Jesus' assumption into heaven is Acts 1:9–11:

> And after He had said these things, He was lifted up while they were looking on, and a cloud received Him out of their sight. And as they were gazing intently into the sky while He was going, behold, two men in white clothing stood beside

them. They also said, "Men of Galilee, why do you stand looking into the sky? This Jesus, who has been taken up from you into heaven, will come in just the same way as you have watched Him go into heaven."

This affirms that it was a literal, visible ascension of His resurrected body. Some have suggested that His body was transformed into being invisible. But the text clearly states, "He was lifted up while they were looking on, and a cloud received Him out of their sight."

This does raise the question of where is Jesus presently. Evangelicals have offered two views. One is that He moved literally and physically into another dimension. This seems to be suggested when Jesus appeared and disappeared after His resurrection (Luke 24:31) and modern physics with its many dimensions, makes this a possibility. The other view is that Jesus is still present in the space–time dimension, just hidden from our view. This seems to have support from the text that says He gradually disappeared and was hidden by a cloud, as opposed to immediately disappearing. Whichever view is held, Christ must still exist in the numerically same physical body, now glorified, in which He died, rose, and ascended.

CHRIST'S PRESENT PRIESTLY SESSION

Jesus at present also preforms an important priestly session for believers. Satan is the accuser of God's people (Rev. 12:8–10) but as John says, "My little children, I am writing these things to you so that you may not sin. And if anyone sins, we have an Advocate with the Father, Jesus Christ the righteous" (1 John 2:1–2). Jesus Christ is our Advocate who pleads the efficacy of His blood, shed for our sins.

Because of Christ's humanity as well as deity, He can sympathize with our human frailties Hebrew 4:14–15 (cf. Heb. 7:17–26) says:

> Therefore, since we have a great high priest who has passed through the heavens, Jesus the Son of God, let us hold fast our confession. For we do not have a high priest who cannot sympathize with our weaknesses, but One who has been tempted in all things as we are, yet without sin.

Since Jesus was tempted in all points that we are, He can, by His present session, overcome these temptations. Paul says,

> No temptation has overtaken you but such as is common to man; and God is faithful, who will not allow you to be tempted beyond what you are able, but with the temptation will provide the way of escape also, so that you will be able to endure it. (1 Cor. 10:13).

The way out is provided by Christ's present intercession for us. This is His present priestly ministry on our behalf.

His ascension (Acts 1:9–11) and session (1 John 2:1–2), also predicted, assured the finished work of redemption and forgiveness (Heb. 1:3; 12:2), and marks the beginning of His invisible reign (1 Peter 3:21, 22) as King someday to be made visible (second coming) and the judgments to follow (Rev. 5:6–14; 11:15; 19:11–21; 20:4–15).

SUMMARY

The study of the Doctrine of Christ (Christology) shows that Jesus of Nazareth alone is eternally the Son of God who appeared in a Preincarnate state at various times in the Old Testament. His anticipation in the Old shows the importance of His virgin birth which is realized in the New. His miracles and sinless life point to His absolute uniqueness. He is affirmed in the New Testament as having all the attributes of man and all the attributes of God. This is explained as the hypostatic union, that Jesus is the Second Person of the Trinity, subsisting without division or mixture in two natures, one human and one divine. Hence, only Jesus' death can be vicarious and His bodily resurrection and ascension provide us with an advocate before the Father that ensures our eternal life.

Questions to Answer

1. What are the biblical verses, from the Old and New Testament that support the substitutionary nature of the atonement?

2. What is the significance of Jesus' bodily assumption into heaven?

3. What is the significance of Jesus' present session in heaven?

Appendix A:

The Trinity

G od is not only a unity (see Geisler, *The Doctrine of God*), He is also a tri–unity; that is there is not only one God (Monotheism), but there are three persons in the one God. This is the orthodox teaching of the Trinity.

The word *Trinity* means God is a plurality within unity. God has a plurality of persons and a unity of essence; God is three persons in one nature. There is only one "What" (essence) in God, but there are three "Whos" (persons) in that one "What." God is three "I's" in His one "It"—there are three Subjects in one Object.

BIBLICAL BASIS

The Trinity or tri–unity of God is a theological mystery arrived at through a study of Scripture. It cannot be argued for the way God's existence is argued for (Appendix B). In addition to teaching that God is one in nature or essence, the Bible also teaches that there are three distinct persons who are God. All are called God and have essential characteristics of persons. Personhood is understood as one who has intellect, feelings, and will. All these characteristics are attributed to each member of the Trinity in Scripture. All three members of the Trinity are persons. Each is referred to as a person ("He"). God the Father has the power of *intellect* to know (Matt. 6:32); the *emotional* faculty to feel (Gen. 6:6); and the power of will to choose (Matt. 6:9–10). The Son too has intellect (John 2:25); feeling (John 11:35) and will (John 6:38). The Holy Spirit also has the elements of personhood. He has a mind (John 14:26); a will (1 Cor. 12:11) and feeling (Eph. 4:30). Each member also has the ability to communicate (Matt. 11:25) and to teach (John 7:16–17) which are personal traits as well.

From Scripture, we read that there is only one God (Deut. 6:4) that the Father (John 6:27), the Son (John 8:58), and the Holy Spirit (Acts 5:3–4) are assigned the names, the attributes, and the acts that can only belong to God (John 1:1–18).

The Father is God

Jesus called "God the Father" (John 6:27) who has a will to be obeyed. Jesus' prayer, "My Father, if this cannot pass away unless I drink it, Your will be done." (Matt. 26:42; John 5:19). Paul recognized "God our Father" (Rom. 1:7) who can do what only God can do: "God the Father, who raised Him [Jesus Christ] from the dead" (Gal. 1:1).

The Son is God

The Son claims to be Yahweh (Jehovah). Yahweh (YHWH) or Jehovah is the special name given by God for Himself. It is revealed to Moses in Exodus 3:14 when God said, "I AM WHO I AM" Other names, "Lord" for example, may be used even of men (Gen. 18:12), but not "I AM WHO I AM." Such a name is reserved only for the one true God. Yet, this is precisely the name Jesus claimed in John 8:58: "Jesus said to them, 'Truly, truly, I say to you, before Abraham was born, I am.'" This statement not only claims existence before Abraham, but equality with the "I AM" of Exodus. The Jews around Him understood His meaning and picked up stones to kill Him for this blaspheming (cf. John 10:31–33).

Jesus also claimed to be equal with God in John 5:18: "For this reason therefore the Jews were seeking all the more to kill Him, because He not only was breaking the Sabbath, but also was calling God His own Father, making Himself equal with God." Jesus forgave sins, which was recognized as something only God could do (Mark 2:5f.). Likewise, the Old Testament teaches that only God is the Giver of life (1 Sam. 2:6), yet Jesus claimed the power to raise the dead in John 5:21: "For just as the Father raises the dead and gives them life, even so the Son also gives life to whom He wishes" (cf. John 5:25, 29).

The Old Testament forbids worshiping anyone other than God (Ex. 20:1–5). The New Testament agrees, showing that men and angels refused worship (Acts 14:13–15; Rev. 2:8–9). But Jesus accepted worship as God on numerous occasions (Matt. 9:18, 14:33, 15:25, 20:20; John 9:38, 20:28),

Jesus repeatedly put His words on a par with God's word "You have heard that the ancients were told, . . . But I say to you" (Matt. 5:21–22). Jesus said, "All authority has been given to Me in heaven and on earth. Go therefore and make disciples of all the nations, baptizing them in the name of the Father and the Son and the Holy Spirit" (Matt. 28:18–19). God gave the Ten Commandments to Moses, but Jesus said, "A new commandment I give to you, that you love one another" (John 13:34). Clearly Jesus expected His words to have equal authority with God's declarations in the Old Testament.

Jesus not only asked people to believe in Him and obey His commandments, but He also asked them to pray in His name: "Whatever you ask in My name, that will I do, so that the Father may be glorified in the Son. If you ask Me anything in My name, I will do it" (John 14:13–14). Jesus even insisted, "no one comes to the Father but through Me." (John 14:6). The disciples prayed *in* Jesus' name (1 Cor 5:4) and *to* Him (Acts 7:59).

Also, it is a teaching of Jesus Christ who prayed to the Father (John 17) and promised the Holy Spirit (John 14–16).

The Holy Spirit is God

The Holy Spirit is referred to as God and Lord. Peter said, "Ananias, why has Satan filled your heart to lie to the Holy Spirit . . . You have not lied to men but to God" (Acts 5:3–4; 1 Cor. 3:16, 6:19). Paul said, "Now the Lord is the Spirit, and where the Spirit of the Lord is, there is liberty" (2 Cor. 3:17).

The Holy Spirit has all the attributes of God such as omniscience (1 Cor. 2:11); omnipresence (Ps. 139:7); eternality (Heb. 9:14), holiness (Eph. 4:30); truth (John 16:13) and life (Rom. 8:2).

The Holy Spirit performs the acts of God, which are also attributed to the Father and the Son. These include creation (Gen. 1:2; Job 33:4); the acts of redemption (Isa. 63:10–11; Eph. 4:30), the performance of miracles (Gal. 3:2–5; cf. Heb. 2:4) and the giving of supernatural gifts (Acts 2:4; 1 Cor. 12:4–11).

The Holy Spirit is associated with God in prayers. The benediction of 2 Corinthians 13:14 contains all three members of the Godhead: "The grace of the Lord Jesus

Christ, and the love of God, and the fellowship of the Holy Spirit, be with you all."

All three persons are together at once. In the Old Testament all three are implied in Isaiah 63:7–10 that says, "I shall make mention of the loving kindnesses of the Lord, the praises of the Lord, According to all that the Lord [Father] has granted us, . . . So He became their Savior [Son]. In all their affliction He was afflicted, and the angel of His presence saved them; In His love and in His mercy He redeemed them, . . . But they rebelled And grieved His Holy Spirit." At Jesus' baptism Matthew 3:16–17 says, After being baptized, Jesus [Son] came up immediately from the water; and behold, the heavens were opened, and he saw the Spirit of God [Holy Spirit] descending as a dove and lighting on Him, and behold, a voice out of the heavens [Father] said, "This is My beloved Son, in whom I am well–pleased." Likewise, Jesus gives the baptismal formula "Go therefore and make disciples of all the nations, baptizing them in the name of the Father and the Son and the Holy Spirit (Matt. 28:19).

THEOLOGY OF THE TRINITY

Hence, all three must be the one (undivided) divine nature. The argument goes as follows:

1) There is only One God.
2) Three different Persons are God: Father, Son, and Holy Spirit.
3) Therefore, all three are the One God.

This does not mean that there are three gods (Tritheism) and this does not mean that God has three modes of existence (modalism). It does mean that God is triune or plurality within unity: three persons in one essence or nature.

God can have only one essence. By "essence" or "nature" is meant what something is. An essence has essential and accidental characteristics. Essential characteristics are necessary, such as a human being must possess rationality. Accidental characteristics are not necessary, such as skin color for a human.

Hence, it is possible to have more than one person in one essence. There is no contradiction in having three persons in one essence. The law of non–contradiction mandates that for two propositions to be contradictory they must affirm and deny something of 1) the same thing; 2) at the same time; and 3) in the same sense (or same relationship). Clearly this is not the case in affirming 1) God is one and only one in relation to His essence and 2) God is more than one (viz., three) in relation to His persons. These are two different senses or relations. Therefore, the Trinity is not contradictory. It is a mystery, but not a contradiction. It may go beyond reason, but it does not go against reason.

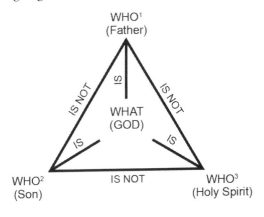

Figure A.1

The term essence (or nature) is appropriately used of God's divinity, since it answers "what" God is. A nature is an objective center of essential attributes. The term person is appropriately applied to God's relations, since it answers "who" God is. A person, as applied to the Trinity, is a subjective center or subsistence of intellect and will. While there can be no differences in God's essence because of unity, there can be a relational differences in God's subsistence or intentions. Hence, God is tri-personal. The three persons are distinct (Matt. 3:16–17, 28:19) from each other via a relation and therefore the Father is not the Son, and the Son is not the Holy Spirit, etc. However, the three persons are the one divine nature and not distinguished from it so it can be said the Father is God, the Son is God and the Holy Spirit is God. The relations in God are actually the same as His essence. God is one "What" and three "Whos" (Figure A.1). The Trinity would be a contradiction if it said God is one "What" and three "Whats" or three "Whos" and one "Who," that is one Nature in three natures, or three persons in one Person. But saying God is one Nature consisting of three co–equal Persons is not contradictory.

All members of the Trinity are equal in essence, but they do have different *roles*. Hence, there is a functional subordination, but not a subordination of nature, which is the one divine essence. The Father is the Source, Sender, and Planner of salvation. The Son is the Means, Sent One, and Achiever of salvation. The Holy Spirit is the Applier of salvation to believers. He is the one that convicts, convinces, and converts. This functional subordination is essential and eternal. Hence, the Son is an eternal Son (Prov. 30:4; Heb. 1:3). He did not become God's Son; He always was related to God the Father as a Son and always will be (1 Cor. 15:24–28).

Illustrations of the Trinity

No analogy is perfect, since in every analogy there is a similarity and a difference. But there are some good analogies or illustrations for the Trinity. The Trinity is like an equilateral triangle that is one figure yet has three different angles from each other. There is simultaneous three-ness in the oneness. It is like one to the third power: 1^3 (1 x 1 x 1) = 1 There are three ones in One. Another is the trifold nature of love. "God is Love" (John 4:16) and love involves three elements: A lover, a beloved, and a spirit of love. These three are one. Love is something only persons do. A final good illustration is that God is like the relation of my intellect (mind) to its ideas, thoughts, and words. Each is distinct, yet they are united, our words cannot be separated from our ideas, and our mind behind them.

The Trinitarian view is that there are three persons that subsist in the one nature. The Trinity must be defended against heretical views. These include Tritheism that says there are three separate gods in the Godhead; Modalism (or Sabellianism) says God is one person in three roles; Binitarianism says there are only two persons in the Godhead.

	PERSON(S)	NATURE(S)
Trinitarianism	Three	One
Tritheism	Three	Three
Modalism	One	One
Binitarianism	Two	One

Table A.1

Some also have objected that the trinity is not compatible with simplicity (see Geisler, *The Doctrine of God*). However, this objection confuses person and essence. Simplicity refers only to God's essence. Each person is identical to the essence. But in respect to one another each person is mutually distinct and not untied with the others. The relationships in God really exist in Him. But the distinctions are not according to essence, but according to what is relative, namely, to personhood. God is essentially one but relationally three. Relations in God do not entail composition. Therefore, the Trinity and simplicity are not contradictory.

Appendix B:

Argument for the Deity of Jesus Christ & Truth of Christianity

Here we can only sketch out and summarize the argument that is used to show the Deity of Jesus Christ and the truth of Christianity. First we show each point of the argument, followed by a brief summary of the arguments and evidence that supports each point.

1. Truth about reality is knowable.
2. The opposite of true is false.
3. It is true that the theistic God exists.
4. If God exists then miracles are possible.
5. Miracles can be used to confirm a message from God.
6. The New Testament is historically reliable.
7. The New Testament says Jesus claimed to be God.
8. Jesus' claim to be God was miraculously confirmed by:
   a. His fulfillment of many prophecies about Himself;
   b. His sinless and miraculous life;
   c. His prediction and accomplishment of His resurrection
9. Therefore, Jesus is God.
10. Whatever Jesus (who is God) teaches is true.
11. Jesus taught that the Bible is the word of God.
12. Therefore, it is true that the Bible is the word of God (and anything opposed to it is false).

1. TRUTH ABOUT REALITY IS KNOWABLE.

Truth is what corresponds to reality. It is when a statement corresponds to the facts or matches its object. Any other approach is self–defeating. To deny this understanding you have to use this understanding.

Truth can be known. Everyone assumes the objectivity and knowability of truth. All other views of truth fail. Agnosticism (Immanuel Kant) says "no one knows the truth." How do you know that is true? It is a self–defeating claiming to know the truth that we cannot know truth. Skepticism (David Hume) says "doubt everything." This is either self–defeating – skeptical about skepticism or begs the question since it is saying doubt should not be doubted. Post–Modernism (Jacque Derrida) says "We must deconstruct all truth claims and reconstruct them which is never objective truth." Either claims to be true (self–defeating) or makes no truth claim and is therefore not relevant since it ignores truth. Relativism (Alfred North Whitehead) says "All truth is changing or in process." Either affirms relativism is absolutely true or is unsuccessful since it is just another relative statement. "It's true for you but not for me" Is that true for you but not for me?

2. THE OPPOSITE OF TRUE IS FALSE.

The law of non–contradiction states opposite ideas cannot both be true at the same time and in the same sense – is undeniable. Since everything cannot be false, something must be true. The true view must correspond to reality. Since opposites cannot both be true, all religions cannot be true since they hold opposing views on crucial differences: God, humanity, Jesus, Death of Christ, Bible, and salvation. If Christianity is true, everything in any other religion that opposes Christianity is false. All truth is narrow, since its opposite is false. One religion can be true. A false religion can have a system with some truth in it. God has provided everyone basic truth about Himself through creation.

3. IT IS TRUE THAT THE THEISTIC GOD EXISTS.

If God does not exist...miracles are not possible, truth is not absolute, morals are not absolute, the Bible is not credible, and life has no ultimate purpose. God is a Supernatural Being who alone is All Powerful, All Intelligent, Morally Perfect, and Creator of the world who can intervene in the world. The following are just outlines of the major arguments used to demonstrate the existence of God.

The cosmological argument comes in two types: First, the horizontal form:

1) Everything that begins had a cause.

2) The universe had a beginning

3) Therefore, the universe had a cause.

Second, the vertical form:

1) Something Exists (e.g., I do).

2) Nothing cannot produce something.

3) Therefore, something exists eternally and necessarily.

4) I am not a necessary and eternal being (since I change).

5) Therefore, both God (a Necessary Being) and I (a contingent being) exist (=theism).

The teleological argument has two types: First, from Astronomy (Anthropic Principle):

1) Anticipatory design shows an intelligent Designer.

2) Human life shows anticipatory design.

3) Hence, Human life shows an intelligent Designer.

Second from micro–biology which uses information the-
ory and intelligent design:

    1) Specified complexity (or Irreducible complexity) has
       an intelligent Designer.

    2) Life has specified complexity (or Irreducible com-
       plexity).

    3) Hence, life had an intelligent Designer.

The moral argument is as follows:

    1) Every law has a law giver.

    2) There is an absolute moral law.

    3) Therefore, there must be an absolute moral law giver.

Finally, the religious need argument:

    1) All persons need God (Theists and Atheists admit).

    2) What we really need really exists.

    3) Therefore, God exists.

The God of our argument must be the same God of the
Bible. Since the same God of Scripture is pure Existence
– Ex. 3:14 "I AM WHO I AM": One (Deut. 6:4), Infinite
(Ps. 147:5), Personal (Gen. 1:26; 2 Cor. 6:18), Morally
Perfect (Ps 86:5; Luke 18:19), Omniscience (Ps. 147:5;
Rom. 11:33), Omnipotent (Gen. 1:1; Matt. 19:26),
Eternal/Necessary (Ps. 90:2; Heb. 1:2), Immutable (Mal.
3:6; Heb. 6:18), Infinite and Omnipresent (1 Kings. 8:27;
Col. 1:17).

4. IF GOD EXISTS THEN MIRACLES ARE POSSIBLE.

It is important to know what miracles are not. They
are not anomalies which have unknown natural causes.
They are not providential which are rare or unusually
events with natural causes. They are not psychological
or only mental projections. They are not magic or tricks
of the senses. And they are not Satanic power, that is
produced by the power unseen but created evil spiritual
creatures. A miracle by definition is a divine intervention

in the natural world that produces an event that would not have resulted from purely natural causes. The primary purpose (not exclusive) is to confirm a message from God (Jn. 3:2, Acts 2:22; Heb. 2:3). The possibility and credibility of miracles is established as follows:

1. If the world had a beginning, then it had a Beginner.
2. The world had a beginning.
3. Therefore, the world had a Beginner.
4. Creation is the biggest miracle of all.
5. If God can do greater miracles (creation) then he can do lesser miracles. (a) If he can create matter, he can multiply matter. (b) If he can bring life to dead matter, he can bring life back to a dead corpse.

5. MIRACLES CAN BE USED TO CONFIRM A MESSAGE FROM GOD.

All three theistic religions hold God can communicate to people and performs miracles. The argument is as follows:

1. If a theistic God exists, then miracles are possible.
2. A miracle is a special act of a theistic God.
3. A theistic God is all–knowing (Omniscient).
4. A theistic God is also a morally perfect Being.
5. An all–knowing, all–perfect God cannot err or deceive (point 3).
6. Hence, a theistic God cannot act to confirm something as true that was false.
7. Therefore, true miracles in connection with a message confirm that message to be from God: (a) the miracle confirms the message, (b) the sign confirms the sermon, (c) an act of God confirms the word of God, and (d) new revelation needs new confirmation.

The criterion of true miracles must include the following:

1. Immediate (Mt. 8:3).
2. Multiple (Acts 1:3).

3. Connected with a truth claim in the name of God (Mk. 2:10–11).

4. Some predictive element (Jn. 13:19).

6. THE NEW TESTAMENT IS HISTORICALLY RELIABLE.

The New Testament (NT) documents are copied accurately. The NT has more, earlier and accurately copied manuscripts than any other book from the ancient world. NT has 5,800 Greek Manuscripts (MSS) vs. *Iliad* that has 1,800 MSS. The gap between the original and the extant MSS 25 (fragments) to 100 yrs. (complete MSS) vs. Homer 400 to 1000 (most MSS) years. The accuracy: Difference in form but not content: *Iliad* of Homer is 95% compared with the NT which is 98–99.9%. The events were recorded accurately. The NT has more writers, earlier and more accurate writings, than any other book from the ancient world. Eleven writers, start between 33 AD (Jesus' death) and 56 AD (Paul). The Gospels Luke–Acts by 62 AD, with Matthew and Mark earlier. There are hundreds of details verified from Luke–Acts: 1. Minute geographical details known to the readers, 2. Specialized details known only to special groups, 3. Specifics of not widely known routes, places, and officials, 4. Correlation of dates in Acts with general history, 5. Details appropriate to that period but not others, 6. Events which reflects a sense of "immediacy." 7. Idioms and culture that bespeak of a first–hand awareness, 8. Verification of numerous details of times, people, and events of that period best known by contemporaries.

All the NT was completed during the lives of eyewitnesses. These eyewitnesses prevent myths that can remove the core historical truth. Paul confirms 27 Gospel events (55–57 AD): Jewish ancestry of Jesus (Gal. 3:16);

His Davidic descent (Rom. 1:3); His virgin birth (Gal. 4:4); His life under Jewish law (Gal. 4:4); His brothers (1 Cor. 9:5); His twelve disciples (1 Cor. 15:7), one of whom was named James (1 Cor. 15:7); that some had wives (1 Cor. 9:5), and that Paul knew Peter and James (Gal. 1: 18–2:16); Jesus' poverty (2 Cor. 8:9); His meekness and gentleness (2 Cor. 10:1); His abuse by others (Rom. 15:3); His teachings on divorce and remarriage (1 Cor. 7:10–11); His view on paying wages of ministers (1 Cor. 9:14); His view on paying taxes (Rom. 13:67); His command to love one's neighbors (Rom. 13:9); On Jewish ceremonial uncleanness (Rom. 14:14); On Jesus' titles of deity (Rom. 1:3–4; 10:9); His institution of the Lord's Supper (1 Cor. 11:23–25); His sinless life (2 Cor. 5:2); His death on the cross (Rom. 4:25; 5:8; Gal. 3:13; 1 Cor. 15:3), specifically by crucifixion (Rom. 6:6; Gal. 2:20), His burial (1 Cor. 15:4); His resurrection on the "third day" (1 Cor. 15:4); His post–resurrection appearance to the Apostles (1 Cor. 15:5–8); His post–resurrection appearances to others (1 Cor. 15:6); His present position at God's right hand (Rom. 8:34).

Non–Christian sources corroborate 12 events known to parallel Gospels: 1. Jesus was from Nazareth, 2. He lived a virtuous life, 3. He performed unusual feats, 4. He introduced new teaching contrary to Judaism, 5. He was crucified under Pontius Pilate, 6. His disciples believed He rose from the dead, 7. His disciples denied polytheism, 8. His disciples worshiped Him, 9. His teachings and disciples spread rapidly, 10. His followers believed they were immortal, 11. His followers had contempt for death, 12. His followers renounced material goods.

No archaeological discovery has controverted a biblical reference.

7. THE NEW TESTAMENT SAYS JESUS CLAIMED TO BE GOD.

The Old Testament (OT) basis includes Jesus claimed the Jewish Messiah is God (Isa. 9:6; 45:6; Psa. 110:1; Zech. 12:10). Jesus quoted Psa 110:1 "The Lord said to My Lord" (Mt. 22). And asked how can the son be Lord at the same time? The only possible answer is that he is both God and Man.

The NT basis includes Jesus claimed to be the "I AM" [of Ex 3:14]. "Most assuredly, I say to you, before Abraham was, I AM" (Jn. 8:58). Jesus accepted worship on ten occasions which is due only to God (Mt. 4:10): 1) The mother of James and John (Mt. 20:20); 2) The Gerasene demoniac (Mk. 5:6); 3) A healed blind man (Jn. 9:38); 4) Doubting Thomas (Jn. 20:28); 5) The women at the tomb (Mt. 28:9); 6) A Canaanite woman (Mt. 15:25); 7) His disciples after the storm (Mt. 14:33); 8) A healed leper (Mt. 8:2); 9) A rich young ruler (Mt. 9:18); 10) Disciples at the Great Commission (Mt. 28:17). The Bible forbids the worshiping of anyone but God (Ex. 20:1–4; Deut. 5:6–9). Jesus placed his words on the same level as God's word, "Heaven and earth will pass away, but my words will by no means pass away" (Mt. 24:35).

8. JESUS' CLAIM TO BE GOD WAS MIRACULOUSLY CONFIRMED BY:

a. His fulfillment of many prophecies about Himself;

There are over 100 Messianic prophecies. Some of the most important include:

1. Seed of the woman (Gen. 3:15).
2. Line of Seth (Gen. 4:25).
3. Descendent of Shem (Gen. 9:26).
4. Offspring of Abraham (Gen. 12:3).
5. Tribe of Judah (Gen. 49:10).
6. From the House of David (2 Sam. 7:12; Jer. 23:5–6).
7. Son of a Virgin (Isa. 7:14).
8. Born in Bethlehem (Micah 5:2).
9. He would die in 33 A.D. Daniel says, "So you are to know and discern that from the issuing of a decree to restore and rebuild Jerusalem [444 B.C.], until Messiah the Prince [A.D. 33], there will be seven weeks and sixty–two weeks [69x7=483]. (Dan. 9:24–25). This is 483 Jewish lunar years (of 360 days each). Add to this 6 more years for the five extra days for 483 years, and it is exactly 483 years (477 + 6) from 444 B.C. to 33 A.D.
10. He would suffer and die for our sins (Isa. 53:5–12).
11. His side would be pierced (Zech. 12:10).
12. He would rise from the dead (Psa. 16:10; Isa. 53:10; Psa. 2:2, 6–7).

The mathematical probability of just nine (9) prophecies coming true of Christ is 1 in 10^{76}. Consider that just 1 in 10^{17} is like finding one grain of sand in a domed football stadium filled with sand. 1 in 10^{76} is like picking the same grain of sand four times in succession.

b. His sinless and miraculous life;

Jesus was without sin. Hebrews says, "For we [have]... One who has been tempted in all things as we are, yet without sin." (Heb. 4:15). Peter says, "He committed no sin, nor was any deceit found in His mouth" (1 Peter 2:22; 1:193:18). John says, "He is righteous" (1 Jn. 2:29). "He is pure" (1 Jn. 3:3). Paul says, "[God] made Him who knew no sin to be sin on our behalf..." (2 Cor. 5:21). Jesus asked, "Which of you convicts me of sin?" (Jn. 8:46).

His enemies and others recognized his innocence a) Judas "I have sinned by betraying innocent blood" (Mt. 27:4). b) Pilate "I am innocent of this Man's blood" (Mt. 27:24). c) Pilate's Wife "Have nothing to do with that righteous Man..." (Mt. 27:19). d) Centurion "Certainly this man was innocent" (Lk. 23:47) and "Truly this was the Son of God!" (Mt. 27:54). e) The thief on the Cross, "Jesus, remember me when you come into your kingdom" (Lk. 23:42). f) Herodians "Teacher, we know that You are truthful and teach the way of God in truth, and defer to no one; for You are not partial to any" (Mt. 22:16).

Jesus proved to be the Son of God by numerous miracles (over 60 in the Gospels): Walking on water, Turning water to wine, Multiplying loaves, Healing a man born blind, Raising a decaying body, Resurrecting Himself , Healing Peter's mother–in–law, Healing many illnesses, Healing ten lepers, Healing a paralytic, Healing a centurion's servant, Casting out demons, Healing an infirmed woman, Healing a man with dropsy, Healing the two blind men, Withering the fig tree, Restoring a servant's ear, Healing a Nobleman's son, Healing a withered hand.

Jesus' teaching, life, and character also shows he is unique. Jesus taught the highest ethic in Sermon on the Mount (Mt. 5–7): 1. The Golden Rule (7:12); 2. Do not judge others (7:1); 3. Love your enemies (5:44); 4. Do not retaliate (5:38–39); 5. Don't be a hypocrite (7:5); 6. Don't lust in your heart (5:27); 7. Be merciful (5:7); 8. Keep your word (5:37); 9. Help the poor (6:3–4); 10. Forgive others (6:12); 11. Don't make money your God (6:24).

Jesus lived the highest ethic: a) Jesus loved little children (Mk. 10:13–14), b) Wept over death of a friend (Jn. 11:35), c) Set the example of servant hood by washing the disciple's feet (Jn. 13:1f.), d) He lived a life of poverty (Mt. 8:20), e) He healed the ear of one of the mob who came to crucify him (Lk. 22:51), f) He loved and chose as a man he knew would betray him (Mt. 10:4; Jn. 17:12), g) He never spoke in his own defense, even against false accusations (Mt. 27:12–14), h) He died for his enemies (Rom. 5:8–10), i) He forgave his crucifiers (Lk. 23:34).

Jesus' character was impeccable; his deeds were un-impeachable, and his life was unsurpassable.

c. His prediction and accomplishment of His resurrection

Jesus predicted his physical death and resurrection. "Behold, we are going up to Jerusalem; and the Son of Man will be delivered to the chief priests and scribes, and they will condemn Him to death, and will hand Him over to the Gentiles to mock and scourge and crucify Him, and on the third day He will be raised up" (Mt. 20:18–19; 16:21 cf. Mk. 9:30–31; 10:33).

Jesus' death is confirmed by the nature of his wounds involved whipping, crucifixion and a spear in the side en-sured death (Mk. 15; Jn. 18). No one survives Roman cru-cifixion: death by asphyxiation. His mother, friends and closest disciple(s) witnessed his death (Mk. 15:40; Jn. 19:25–26; Lk. 22:54). Everyone, friend and foe, had vest-ed interest in knowing it was Jesus on the cross that died. The Romans were professional executioners who pro-nounced Jesus dead (Jn. 19:33). Pilate double–checked to make sure Jesus was dead (Mk. 15:45). The Jews never denied the account of his dead body being buried in the tomb of Joseph of Arimathea, a member of Sanhedrin (Jn. 19:38). Non–Christian (1st–2nd Cen.) writers re-corded Jesus' death: Josephus, Tacitus, Thallus, Lucian,

Phelgon, and the Jewish Talmud. Modern medical authorities examined the ancient process of crucifixion.

The evidence that Jesus rose from the dead is substantial. Jesus' tomb was found empty with grave clothes in it (Jn. 20:6–8; 17). Over 500 witnesses saw him over 12 times. Touching is mentioned twice and was offered twice. They saw His crucifixion scars: 1. Mary (Jn. 20:10–18); 2. Mary & Women (Mt. 28:1–10); 3. Peter (1 Cor. 15:5); 4. Two Disciples (Lk. 24:13–35); 5. Ten Apostles (Lk. 24:36–49; Jn. 20:19–23); 6. Eleven Apostles (Jn. 20:24–31); 7. Seven Apostles (Jn. 21); 8. All Apostles (Mt. 28:16–20; Mk. 16:14–18); 9. 500 Brethren (1 Cor. 15:6); 10. James (1 Cor. 15:7); 11. All Apostles (Acts 1:4–8); 12. Paul (Acts 9:1–9; 1 Cor. 15:8)

The evidence of a physical resurrection is also compelling. The empty tomb shows the same physical body in the tomb permanently vacated it alive three days later (Mt. 28:6). The resurrection body had "flesh and bones" (Lk. 24:39). Jesus was touched by Mary (Jn. 20:17), and the women (Mt. 28:9). Jesus revealed crucifixion scars to disciples (Lk. 24:39) and Thomas to touch him (Jn. 20:27). Jesus ate physical food four times (Lk. 24:30; 24:42–43; Jn. 21:12–13; Acts 1:4). He was seen with the naked eye (Mt. 28:17) and heard with natural ears (Jn. 20:15–16). The term *body* (soma) always means physical body in the NT of an individual (1 Cor. 15:44).

9. THEREFORE, JESUS IS GOD.

Because Jesus' resurrection proves his claim to be God is true, it follows that everything Jesus affirms is true is true.

10. WHATEVER JESUS (WHO IS GOD) TEACHES IS TRUE.

Jesus affirmed many things about the Bible, Old Testament, that are true.

11. JESUS TAUGHT THAT THE BIBLE IS THE WORD OF GOD.

The Bible is divinely authoritative. Jesus said "It is written . . ." in a present imperative, still existing written authority (Mt. 4:4, 7, 10). It is imperishable. "For truly I say to you, until heaven and earth pass away, not the smallest letter or stroke shall pass from the Law until all is accomplished" (Mt. 5:17–18). It is infallible. Jesus said, "Scripture cannot be broken" (Jn. 10:35).

It is inerrant (without error). Jesus taught: "You are in error because you do not know the Scriptures or the power of God" (Mt. 22:29). Implies the Scriptures are not in error. Jesus prayed: "Thy Word is truth" (Jn. 17:17).

The Bible must be inerrant because:
1) The Bible is the word of God.
2) God cannot err.
3) Therefore, the Bible cannot err.

To deny this reasoning you must either hold 1) that the Bible is not the word of God or 2) that God can err (Mt. 4:4; Rom. 3:4; Jn. 17:17; Jn. 10:35). If not, then you must conclude that the Bible cannot err.

It is historically reliable (Mt. 12:40; Mt. 24:37–38). Jesus and his Apostles affirmed the OT:

1. Creation of the universe (Gen. 1) Jn. 1:3; Col. 1:16.

2. Creation of Adam and Eve (Gen. 1–2) 1Tim. 2:13–14.

3. Marriage of Adam and Eve (Gen. 1–2) 1Tim. 2:13.

4. Temptation of the woman (Gen. 3) 1Tim. 2:14.

5. Disobedience and sin of Adam (Gen. 3) Rom. 5:12; 1 Cor. 15:22.

6. Sacrifices of Abel and Cain (Gen. 4) Heb. 11:4.

7. Murder of Abel by Cain (Gen. 4) 1 Jn. 3:12.

8. Birth of Seth (Gen. 4) Lk. 3:38.

9. Translation of Enoch (Gen. 5) Heb. 11:5.

10. Marriage before the flood (Gen. 6) Lk. 17:27.

11. The flood and destruction of man (Gen. 7) Mt. 24:39.

12. Preservation of Noah and his family (Gen. 8–9) 2 Peter 2:5.

13. Genealogy of Shem (Gen. 10) Lk. 3:35–36.

14. Birth of Abraham (Gen. 11) Lk. 3:34.

15. Call of Abraham (Gen. 12–13) Heb. 11:8.

16. Tithes to Melchizedek (Gen. 14) Heb. 7:1–3.

17. Justification of Abraham (Gen. 15) Rom. 4:3.

18. Ishmael (Gen. 16) Gal. 4:21–24.

19. Promise of Isaac (Gen. 17) Heb. 11:18.

20. Lot and Sodom (Gen. 18–19) Lk. 17:29.

21. Birth of Isaac (Gen. 21) Acts 7:9–10.

22. Offering of Isaac (Gen. 22) Heb. 11:17.

23. The burning bush (Ex. 3:6) Lk. 20:32.

24. Exodus through the Red Sea (Ex. 14:22) 1 Cor. 10:1–2.

25. Provision of water and manna (Ex. 16:4; 17:6) 1 Cor. 10:3–5.

26. Lifting up serpent in the wilderness (Num. 21:9) Jn. 3:14.

27. Fall of Jericho (Joshua 6:22–25) Heb. 11:30

28. Miracles of Elijah (1Kings 17:1; 18:1) Jas. 5:17.

29. Jonah in the great fish (Jonah 2) Mt. 12:40.

30. Three Hebrew youths in furnace (Dan. 3) Heb. 11:34.

31. Daniel in lion's den (Dan. 6) Heb. 11:33.

32. Slaying of Zechariah (2 Chron. 24:20–22) Mt. 23:35.

It is scientifically accurate. Jesus taught from Genesis: "[God] . . . made them at the beginning 'male and female.'" (Mt. 19:4–5). It has ultimate supremacy. "[Jesus] answered and said to them, "Why do you yourselves transgress the commandment of God for the sake of your tradition... And by this you invalidated the word of God for the sake of your tradition" (Mt. 15:3, 6).

Jesus confirmed the OT explicitly and the NT implicitly by promising the Holy Spirit. "But the Helper, the Holy Spirit, whom the Father will send in My name, He will teach you all things and bring to your remembrance all things I said to you" (Jn. 14:26). "However, when He, the Spirit of truth, has come, He will guide you into all truth; for He will not speak on His own authority, but whatever He hears He will speak, and He will tell you things to come" (Jn. 16:13). If the Bible is not the word of God, then Jesus is not the Son of God. If Jesus is the Son of God, then the Bible is the word of God.

12. THEREFORE, IT IS TRUE THAT THE BIBLE IS THE WORD OF GOD (AND ANYTHING OPPOSED TO IT IS FALSE).

This does not mean: There is no truth outside the Bible. The OT mentions The Book of Jasher (Josh. 10:13), references the Chronicles of Samuel, Nathan, and Gad the Seer (1 Chron. 29:29). The NT says, "Now there were many other things that Jesus did" (Jn. 21:25; cf.

20:31), Jude 14–15 references The Book of Enoch, Paul quotes three pagan authors: 1) Aratus in Acts 17:28b; 2) Epimenides of Crete in Titus 1:12 also in Acts 17:28a and 3) Meander in 1 Cor. 15:33. Truth is found in the physical sciences, mathematics, social sciences, history, and personal experiences. *Sola Scripture* does not mean the Bible is the only source of truth (Rom. 1, 2). *Sola Scripture* does mean the Bible is the only written source of infallible truth from God.

This does not mean there is no truth in other religions. There are moral similarities in Religions:

"I have not slain men" (Ancient Egyptian).

"Utter not a word by which anyone could be wounded" (Hindu).

"Men were brought into existence...that they might do one another good" (Roman).

"He whose heart is in the smallest degree set upon goodness will dislike no one" (Ancient Chinese).

He "who mediates oppression, his dwelling is overturned" (Babylonian).

"Natural affection is a thing right and according to Nature" (Greek).

"I saw in Nastrond [=Hell]...beguilers of others' wives" (Old Norse).

"If a native made a 'find' of any kind and marked it, it was thereafter safe for him...no matter how long he left it" (Australian Aborigines).

"Do not do to others what you would not have them do to you" (Negative Golden Rule: Confucius).

There are theological truths in other religions: The Theistic God exists is affirmed by Judaism, Islam, and pre–literate Religions. Most or many religions hold humans have a soul, Immortality (life after death), resurrection, basic moral laws, "Prayer" (meditation) to God. Many show an original Mono–theism that degenerated into various religions with some truth.

This does mean everything taught in the Bible is true. This does mean nothing opposed to what is taught in the Bible is true (point 2). The assertion "truth does not correspond to reality" is a statement that claims to correspond to reality. The Law of Non–contradiction states opposite ideas cannot both be true at the same time and in the same sense. Anyone who says "opposites can both be true" must answer "is the opposite of that true?"

Christianity teaches God is Triune, humans are sinners by nature, Jesus is God and man, he died and rose from the dead, the Bible is not corrupted, and salvation is not by works but a free gift to all who believe. Most religions, such as Islam, deny all these.

This does mean Christianity is the true religion. Everything Christianity teaches is true (Psa. 119:160; Mt. 22:29; Jn. 17:17; Rom. 2:2; 3:4; 2 Tim. 2:15). Christianity's teaching is superior. They are the highest teaching known to man. They are the most comprehensive teachings known. They are the most widespread teaching in the world (the Bible is the all–time best seller). They are the most enduring teaching (withstanding the test of time). Christianity's teaching is sufficient for faith and practice (2 Tim. 3:16–17; Rev. 22:19). Of all human beings, Christ alone is God (Point 7) and he is the only way to God:

"I am the way, and the truth, and the life; no one comes to the Father but through Me" (Jn. 14:6).

"Truly, truly, I say to you, he who does not enter by the door into the fold of the sheep, but climbs up some other way, he is a thief and a robber...I am the door; if anyone enters through Me, he will be saved" (Jn. 10:1, 9).

"For unless you believe that I am he [the Messiah] you will die in your sins" (Jn. 8:24).

"He who believes in Him is not judged; he who does not believe has been judged already, because he has not believed in the name of the only begotten Son of God" (Jn. 3:18).

"And there is salvation in no one else; for there is no other name under heaven that has been given among men by which we must be saved" (Acts 4:12; cf. 1 Tim. 2:5).

Bibliography

Aquinas, Thomas. *Compendium of Theology*. St. Louis: B. Herder Book, 1948.

Aquinas, Thomas. *Summa Theologica.* Translated by Fathers of the English Dominican Province. Vol. 1–5. Allen, TX: Christian Classics, 1948.

Babylonian Talmud, Tosephta Sotah. Peabody, MS: Hendrickson, 2005.

Brown, Harold O. J. *Heresy*. Grand Rapids, Baker Books, 1984.

Calvin, John. *Institutes of the Christian Religion*. 2 vols. Ed. John T. McNeill. Trans. Ford Lewis Battles. In Library of Christian Classics. Vols. 20–20. Eds. John Baillie, John T. McNeill, and Henry P. Van Dusen. Philadelphia: Westminster, 1960.

Chafer, Lewis Sperry. *Systematic Theology*. Vol. 1–2. Abridged Edition. Edited by John F. Walvoord. Wheaton: Victor Books, 1988.

Culver, Robert D. *Systematic Theology: Biblical & Historical*. Bercker, Germany: Mentor, 2005.

Edwards, W. D., et al. "On The Physical Death of Jesus Christ" *Journal of the American Medical Association*, 255:11, March 21, 1986, 1463.

Eusebius. *Ecclesiastical History*. Grand Rapids, MI: Baker, 1990.

Elwell, Walter A., ed. *Topical Analysis of the Bible*. Grand Rapids: Baker, 1991.

Enns, Paul. *The Moody Handbook of Theology*. Rev. ed. Chicago: Moody Press, 2008.

Erickson, Millard. *Christian Theology*. Grand Rapids: Baker, 1991.

Geisler, Norman L. & Douglas E. Potter. *A Popular Survey of Bible Doctrine*, NGIM, 2015.

_____. *A Prolegomena to Evangelical Theology*. NGIM, 2016.

_____. *The Bible: Its Origin, Nature & Collection, NGIM Guide to Bible Doctrine, Vol. 1*, NGIM, 2016.

_____. *The Doctrine of Creation, NGIM Guide to Bible Doctrine, Vol. 4*, NGIM, 2016.

_____. *The Doctrine of God, NGIM Guide to Bible Doctrine, Vol. 2*, NGIM, 2016.

Geisler, Norman L. & J. Kerby Anderson. *Origin Science: A Proposal for the Creation–Evolution Controversy*. Grand Rapids: Baker, 1987.

Geisler, Norman L. & Ron Rhodes. *Conviction without Compromise: Standing Strong in the Core Beliefs of the Christian Faith.* Eugene, Harvest House, 2008.

Geisler, Norman L. & William C. Roach. *Defending Inerrancy*. Grand Rapids: Baker, 2011.

Geisler, Norman L. & William E. Nix. *From God to Us*. Rev. & Exp. Chicago: Moody Press, 2012.

_____. *General Introduction to the Bible*. Rev. ed. Chicago: Moody Press, 1986.

Geisler, Norman L. *A Popular Survey of the New Testament*. Grand Rapids: Baker Books, 2007.

_____. *Creating God in the Image of Man?* Minneapolis: Bethany House, 1997.

_____. *Christ the Theme of the Bible*. Chicago, Moody, 1968.

_____. *Knowing the Truth About Creation*. Ann Arbor: Servant Books, 1989.

_____. *Miracles and the Modern Mind*. Grand Rapids: Baker, 1992.

_____. *Systematic Theology*. Minneapolis: Bethany, 2011.

_____. *The Battle for the Resurrection*. Nashville: Thomas Nelson, 1989.

_____. *Thomas Aquinas: An Evangelical Appraisal*. Grand Rapids: Baker, 1991.

_____. *Twelve Points That Show Christianity is True*. Bastion Books, 2012.

_____., ed. *Inerrancy*. Grand Rapids: Zondervan, 1980.

Gromacki, Robert. *The Virgin Birth: Doctrine of Deity*. Baker, 1981.

Habermas, Gary. *The Historical Jesus: Ancient Evidence for the Life of Christ*. Joplin, College Press, 1996.

Hemer, Colin. *The Book of Acts in the Setting of Hellenistic History*. Eisenbrauns, 1990.

Irenaeus. *Against Heresies.* in *The Ante–Nicene Fathers*. Eerdmans, 1885.

Josephus, *The New Complete Works of Josephus*, translated by William Whiston. Grand Rapids: Kregel, 1966.

Lewis, C. S. *Mere Christianity*. New York: Macmillan, 1943

Lightner, Robert P. *Sin the Savior and Salvation*. Grand Rapids: Kregel, 1991.

_____. *The Death Christ Died: A Biblical Case for Unlimited Atonement*. Kregel, 1998.

Machen, J. Gresham. *The Virgin Birth of Christ*. New York, Harper, 1930.

Nash, Ronald. *The Gospels and the Greeks: Did the New Testament Borrow from Pagan Thought?* Phillipsburg, Presbyterian and Reformed, 2003.

O'Hair, J. C. *The Unsearchable Riches of Christ*, Grand Rapids: Grace, 1976.

Rhodes, Ron. *Christ Before the Manger: The Life and Times of the Preincarnate Christ*. Grand Rapids: Baker Book House, 1992.

Ryrie, Charles. *Basic Theology: A Popular Systematic Guide to Understanding Biblical Truth.* Chicago, Moody, 1999.

Schaff, Philip. *A Select Library of the Nicene and Post–Nicene Fathers of the Christian Church*. Grand Rapids: Eerdmans, 1988–1991.

Wolvoord, John. *Jesus Christ Our Lord.* Chicago: Moody Press, 1980.

Walvoord, John, & Roy Zuck, eds. *The Bible Knowledge Commentary.* Vols. 1–2. Wheaton: Victor, 1987.

Wenham, John. *Christ and the Bible,* 3rd ed. Grand Rapids: Baker, 1994.

NORM GEISLER INTERNATIONAL MINISTRIES

Norm Geisler International Ministries is dedicated to carrying on the life's work of its co-founder, Norman L. Geisler. Described as a cross between Billy Graham and Thomas Aquinas, Norm Geisler, PhD, is a prolific author, professor, apologist, philosopher, and theologian. He has authored or co-authored over 100 books and co-founded 2 seminaries.

NGIM is focused on equipping others to proclaim and defend the Christian Faith by providing evangelism and apologetic training.

More Information

Website:	http://NormGeisler.com
Training:	http://NGIM.org (Norm Geisler International Ministries)
e-Books:	http://BastionBooks.com
Email:	Dr.NormanGeisler@outlook.com
Facebook:	http://facebook.com/normgeisler
Twitter:	https://www.twitter.com/normgeisler
Videos:	http://www.youtube.com/user/DrNormanLGeisler/videos
Biblical Inerrancy:	http://DefendingInerrancy.com
Seminaries:	Southern Evangelical Seminary http://SES.edu
	Veritas Evangelical Seminary http://VES.edu

Other books from

NGIM

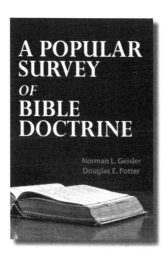

A POPULAR
SURVEY
OF
BIBLE
DOCTRINE

Norman L. Geisler
Douglas E. Potter

CHRISTIANS, more than ever, need a basic introduc-tion to Bible doctrine that is systematic and true to Scripture. This book is a popular introduction to the study of Bible doctrine firmly in the evangelical tradition. Each chapter covers a biblical doctrine, stresses its doc-trinal importance and inter–connectedness to formulat-ing a Christian world view. The study questions provided help reinforce the material and make it usable even for a formal study of Bible doctrine. It is ideal for personal study and in groups for the home, church, school or min-istry environment.

www.NGIM.org

NGIM
Guide to
Bible Doctrine

NGIM Guide to Bible Doctrine Book 1

THIS is a popular introduction to the study of the doctrine of the Bible firmly rooted in the evangelical tradition. Each chapter covers an area of the doctrine of the Bible, stresses its basis, doctrinal importance and interconnectedness to formulating a Christian view of the Bible and other doctrines. The study questions provided help reinforce the material and make it usable even for a formal study of the Bible's nature. It is ideal for personal study or in groups for the home, church, school or ministry environment.

www.NGIM.org

Guide to
Bible Doctrine

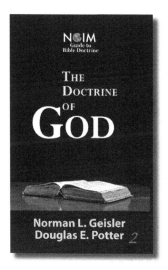

NGIM Guide to Bible Doctrine Book 2

This is a popular introduction to the study of the biblical doctrine of God firmly in the evangelical tradition. Each chapter covers an area of the doctrine of God, stresses its biblical basis, doctrinal importance and interconnectedness to formulating a Christian view of God. The study questions provided help reinforce the material and make it usable even for a formal study of God's nature. It is ideal for personal study or in groups for the home, church, school or ministry environment.

www.NGIM.org

Manufactured by Amazon.ca
Bolton, ON

31087254R00059